"Anyone in a leadership role shou Claudia's well-written and insightfu purpose in today's ever-changing work environment. Insightful, fun, powerful, and witty. Claudia has hit a home run with her creative way of conveying leadership lessons that everyone should consider."

~ George Nahodil, President and CEO
Members 1st Federal Credit Union

"In an evolving workforce environment, Claudia's Frientorship approach challenges leaders to venture out of their own comfort zones to engage with their team members. The book offers perspectives on the principles of Frientorship as well as palpable, tactical suggestions on implementing this fresh culture in an organization. Claudia has delivered this message in a compelling style, using real-life stories that make the book as enjoyable as it is impactful."

~ Fali Sidhva, President and COO
Community Veterinary Partners

"Frientorship goes beyond traditional approaches to employee engagement by focusing on – rather than ignoring – the importance of developing meaningful connections across all leadership levels. Claudia's viewpoint that friendship, guided by leadership and mentorship, enriches the workplace is refreshing and will help any leader learn to leverage the power of relationships."

~ Amanda J. Lavis, Executive Branch
Equal Employment Opportunity Program Manager
State of Hawaii

"Being a leader in today's very challenging environment does not come with easy "how to" instructions. Claudia's Frientorship concept is a way for you to become a more effective and purposeful leader. Her method is a guaranteed pathway to accelerate the potential of your organization."

~ John Dame, Author,
Business Strategist and Leadership Coach

"Claudia's ability to connect through storytelling is a true gift. This book is a treasure chest of stories and life lessons woven into a patchwork of impactful insights and resources every leader needs, providing a simple road map to embracing the value of combining friendship, mentorship, and leadership. Plus, a leadership book that quotes rapper Ice Cube to get their point across is a must read for me!"

~ Renee Holloman, SVP and Chief People Officer
Post Acute Medical, LLC

"Through the authentic lens of her own life experiences, Claudia provides the reader a 'growth practice' employee engagement solution that has the potential to save businesses thousands of dollars in employee migration. Frientorship is more than a concept or a practice, though. It is sure to be a cultural movement that every business will aspire to be at the fore!"

~ Jayne Huston, Business Coach and
Women's Professional Organization Chapter Chair

FRIENTORSHIP

Using friendship, mentorship, and leadership to drive profitability and build a sustainable competitive advantage

CLAUDIA WILLIAMS

Copyright © 2018 Claudia Williams

All rights reserved.

Printed in the United States of America.

 Year of the Book
135 Glen Avenue
Glen Rock, PA 17327

No part of this publication may be reproduced or distributed in any form or by any means without the prior permission of the author.

Neither the publisher nor the author is engaged in rendering legal or other professional services through this book. If expert assistance is required, the services of appropriate professionals should be sought. The publisher and the author shall have neither liability nor responsibility to any person or entity with respect to any loss or damage caused directly or indirectly by the information in this publication.

To protect the privacy of certain individuals, some names and identifying details have been changed.

ISBN 13: 978-1-945670-88-6

ISBN 10: 1-945670-88-6

Frientorship® is a registered trademark of The Human Zone LLC and is used with permission.

DEDICATION

For my husband, Steve. My love. My best friend. My rock. The Yin to my Yang. The kind of dad I wish every kid could have.

For my girlies, Marena and Carissa, who make me laugh every single day and who opened up my heart to a love I could not have imagined until they came into my life.

TABLE OF CONTENTS

CHAPTER 1

THE WORKPLACE APOCALYPSE

> *If you choose to not deal with an issue,*
> *then you give up your right of control over the issue*
> *and it will select the path of least resistance.*
>
> *~ Susan Del Gatto*

Do you hear the alarm bells ringing? Now is the time for Corporate America to realize that an epidemic is exploding, and it isn't going away without a cure. Corporate America calls it a lack of "employee engagement." It's a downright, real-life zombie apocalypse. Employees are unhappy at work, and their unhappiness is breeding disengagement.

Consider these alarming statistics. Eight out of ten employees don't like their jobs. Shockingly, 87 percent of employees aren't engaged at work or – even worse – they're actively disengaged.[1] That means they've gotten to the point of saying, "Whatever." Even in a small

---

[1] Gallup Organization, "State of the American Workplace," 2017. http://news.gallup.com/reports/178514/state-american-workplace.aspx

business, one disengaged employee can have a drastic impact on profitability.

Chances are, you've been there, or you've watched it unfold in your co-workers. I remember the day my disengagement hit me like a ton of bricks. I was heading to China for the second time in as many weeks. This time, my boss was going with me. It was 6:30 A.M., and I was standing in my driveway with my husband and our two daughters, then ages seven and nine. We were waiting for my boss to pick me up to head to the airport.

The black Audi from the car service turned into my driveway and came to a stop. The rear passenger side door opened, and my boss slowly exited and walked toward us. This was the first time she would meet my daughters. I was both nervous and excited about how the first impression would go. I made the standard introductions, and my daughters politely shook her hand and said hello.

My then-seven-year-old, Carissa, was looking up at my boss with her big, brown eyes – cute as ever. "Nice to meet you," she said.

This is going really well, I thought.

"So [insert pause while she looked my boss up and down], *you're* the reason my mama's never home."

Bam. I figured I would start packing up my office when I returned from China. But the more I thought about what Carissa said, the more I came to the realization that my boss wasn't the reason I was never home. *I* was the reason I was never home. When I *was* home, I wasn't present. I was on the phone with China or India or answering the hundreds of e-mails I received. There was one week when I had over 1,500 unread e-mails by Friday afternoon, and that was after I tried to read through them every night after back-to-back meetings all day long. I had chosen a job which required that of me. My boss wasn't *making* me do anything.

I then started paying more attention to the people who crossed my path over the course of a workday. I noticed that many of them were in the same boat. I didn't mind hard work, but I was unhappy and often felt isolated both on the job and at home. I was becoming more and more disengaged, going through the motions to try to get things done, and I didn't have anything else left in me after that. I was becoming a zombie (and thanks to sleep deprivation, I looked like one, too).

I knew I wasn't performing my best work, and I knew my attitude wasn't good either. I was in the wrong job for me, and the isolation that came with being extraordinarily busy had taken a toll on my work and personal life.

According to former U.S. Surgeon General, Vivek Murthy, almost half of American adults report feeling lonely, and CEOs are no different.[2] Over half of CEOs report feeling isolated at work, and over half of them believe it negatively impacts their performance.

Murthy explains that the result of loneliness at work is lower performance, limited creativity, and impaired

---

[2] Vivek Murthy, "Work and the Loneliness Epidemic," *Harvard Business Review*, September 2017.

reasoning and decision making. This apocalypse is expensive. Actively disengaged employees cost companies between $450 and $550 billion – BILLION – each year. Employees are zombies, the walking dead, just going through the motions. Individually, their misery is costing them their health, their relationships, and their happiness. The solution, Murthy says, is for companies to do more to foster social interactions among employees at work.

As if the employee zombie apocalypse isn't bad enough, good employees – the ones with the right skills to get the job done and with the potential to lead – are in short supply. Over half of employees today are actively looking for another job at this very moment. And they're doing it right from their phones while they're sitting in business meetings at work.

As of the date of publication of this book, the unemployment rate was lingering around 4.1 percent. When unemployment is low, it becomes increasingly difficult for employers to attract and retain the best people. If the best people don't have a compelling connection and reason to stay, they can find a great job down the street. And they will.

The issue of loneliness and engagement is not a millennial issue; it's a human issue. The research upon which Murthy relied involved adults age forty-five and older. That said, millennials are destined to comprise about 70 percent of the workforce by 2020, yet they are the least engaged of all generations.

Here are the statistics from The Gallup Organization:[3]

MILLENNIALS ARE THE LEAST ENGAGED GENERATION AT WORK

Engaged

MILLENNIALS	GEN XERS	BABY BOOMERS	TRADITIONALISTS
29%	32%	33%	45%

Not Engaged

MILLENNIALS	GEN XERS	BABY BOOMERS	TRADITIONALISTS
55%	50%	48%	41%

Actively Disengaged

MILLENNIALS	GEN XERS	BABY BOOMERS	TRADITIONALISTS
16%	18%	19%	14%

GALLUP

Let's be clear about something. This is not about bashing millennials, who are routinely accused of feeling entitled to everything without working for any of it. It is true that millennials are making demands on today's workplace, but their demands could have been predicted five or ten years ago if companies had been paying attention to the signs.

From the time they were kids, millennials were socialized differently than Generation Xers and Baby Boomers. The gender divide isn't a divide for millennials. Men and women together want the same things out of work and life. It is less about entitlement and more about finding something that feels meaningful and worthwhile. It isn't about the money or going for the highest paycheck. It's about the ultimate human

---

[3] Gallup Organization, "State of the American Workplace," 2017. http://news.gallup.com/reports/178514/state-american-workplace.aspx

experience – the *connection* millennials feel to co-workers, the community, the company, the purpose.

Gallup estimates the cost of millennial turnover alone from lack of engagement is around $30.5 billion each year. For millennials, the problem isn't only workplace engagement. Their leverage as consumers will be larger than any generation which preceded. They are less likely to attach themselves to a specific brand or company than other generations. Millennials want more out of their lives, more out of their jobs, and more bang for their buck.

Gallup studied the relationship between employee engagement and performance across 192 organizations and almost 50,000 business/work units, encompassing some 1.4 million employees. The business units that scored in the top half on employee engagement close to doubled the odds of their success rates compared to the units that scored in the bottom half.

When you consider the demands on the employee and customer experience, it's no surprise that the primary concern identified by CEOs in the U.S. and a top concern for CEOs globally is human capital – the ability to attract and retain the very best, most capable people. Companies with engaged workforces outperform their competitors by 147 percent in earnings per share.

The Conference Board – an independent business membership and research association – issued a report based on its 2018 C-Suite Challenge survey. CEOs and C-suite executives from around the globe answer questions about their most pressing business concerns. The result? *Culture is king.* Companies desperately want to build inclusive, transparent, safe workplace cultures that foster collaboration and innovation. In fact, chief human resources officers identified their number one strategy to build great workplace cultures is to increase accountability by holding leaders responsible for their own behaviors.

Leadership development continues to be a priority, as it should be. You can't build a culture if you aren't building your leaders. If you don't have a great culture, you will never have engaged employees.

Many businesses address culture by spending a lot of time and money developing carefully-crafted workplace policies and procedures. They hang gigantic posters with words like "loyalty" and "integrity" all over the building. They have the right words, and they say the right things at the right time. While these are all ways to reinforce behavior expectations, the words alone do not create or define the culture. If a company really wants to know what its culture is, then the leaders need to ask their team members. They need to listen and be willing to act on the responses.

Thanks to social media, employees with legitimate gripes about workplace culture have global platforms on which to express their concerns. Their social media posts can and do go viral. The feedback and ratings they provide on websites like glassdoor.com cannot be removed by the company. Companies no longer control all forms of media, making it possible for negative messages about leadership and culture to have a huge impact on consumers and jobseekers.

Fostering employee engagement and commitment is what will separate the best companies from... well... everyone else. If we are going to try to build something, we need to know what it is. What *is* employee engagement?

Employee engagement: *A heightened emotional and intellectual connection that an employee has for his/her job, organization, manager, or co-workers that in turn, influences him/her to apply discretionary effort to his/her work.*

~ John M. Gibbons, *Employee Engagement: A Review of Current Literature and Its Implications*, The Conference Board, Research Report, 2006.

A culture of engagement[4] is defined as "a set of accepted organizational values, behaviors and practices that promotes increasing levels of engagement as a cultural norm." At the end of the day, it's about winning employees' hearts and minds.

Winning over hearts and minds is done by building purposeful and meaningful workplace *relationships.* It's the relationship that serves as the foundation for every behavior and action that drives engagement.

Corporate America has either been focusing on the wrong things or failing to link the right things together. For example, they've been focusing on higher compensation and offering more vacation days or installing a big-screen television in the break room or a pool table or treadmill desks. They have been developing wellness programs to help generate a healthier

---

4 Rebecca Ray, PhD, "DNA of Engagement: How Organizations Create and Sustain Highly Engaging Cultures," The Conference Board, Research Report, 2014.

workforce. Each of these things is necessary to be competitive in the marketplace for talent *acquisition*.

When properly combined and utilized, these things also have the power to help drive engagement and reduce absenteeism. The best example is the company who gives a fitness tracker to each new hire during orientation. The utilization rates climb when employees walk together during lunch breaks. They're in it together, getting healthier together and building strong bonds.

Absent the opportunity to bond, no single thing by itself solves the problem that arises after the first day on the job: poor talent *retention*.

Corporate America has been throwing *things* at people to solve the problem instead of realizing that it is *people* who will solve the problem. It is the *people* who will increase utilization rates of wellness programs. It is the *people* who need to have the time to connect with each other in the break room. Without human connection, the value of the benefits and perks cannot be realized.

FRIENTORSHIP FACTS

♦ Poor workplace culture, resulting in a lack of employee engagement, hurts employee productivity and retention and company profitability.

♦ Corporate America has wasted time and money giving employees more "things" to entice them to be happier and more productive without connecting the "things" to the people.

♦ True culture change is driven by building purposeful, meaningful workplace relationships that foster collaboration, innovation and, ultimately, profitability.

CHAPTER 2

FRIENTORSHIP: THE SOLUTION

*The problems are solved, not by giving new information,
but by arranging what we have known since long.*

~ Ludwig Wittgenstein, *Philosophical Investigations*

Whenever a business wants to change something or learn how to do it better, they start to examine industry best practices. Best practices, however, are what other companies have been doing over some period of time that have generated demonstrable results for *them*. Best practices are someone else's *past* practices. And if businesses are only trying to catch up with the past, they're going to miss the future. Instead, they should be thinking about *next* practices, not best practices.

The next practice that will solve the problems of poor culture, workplace loneliness, and lack of employee engagement is *frientorship*. Frientorship is a combination of friendship, mentorship, and leadership, leveraging key principles to teach us how to build meaningful connections with people at work. If leaders leverage these principles, they will make themselves happier and more fulfilled, they will make their teams happier and more fulfilled, and they will be able to cascade these principles throughout their organization to build the kind of connectivity and commitment they desperately need. Happiness breeds engagement. And engagement breeds success. It isn't the other way around.

Many people believe that being friends with employees and building purposeful workplace relationships based on that friendship is a terrible idea, a disaster in the making. Gordon Gekko would probably say this is sentimental gibberish – a misguided, touchy-feely approach to leadership and human resources. In the 1987 original movie, *Wall Street*, Gekko famously said, "Gimme guys that are poor, smart, and hungry. And no feelings. You win a few, you lose a few, but you keep on fighting. If you want a friend, get a dog. It's trench warfare out there, pal."

Gordon isn't the only one who thinks being friends at work is a terrible idea. Inc. Magazine published an article in 2014 called, *"7 Reasons You Can't Be Friends with Your Employees."* The author, Marla Tabaka, explains:

1. "It's not scalable." With all of the different personality types in an organization, you will naturally be drawn to certain people, and inevitably you will play favorites.

2. "They won't take you seriously." Your friends will roll their eyes at decisions you make, and they may not even carry out your directives.

3. "It will complicate your relationships." Friendships get complicated when you're making decisions about compensation and bonuses and work hours

and promotions. You should keep things as simple as possible.

4. "Their personal issues will get in the way." You'll spend too many work hours being a sounding board for personal problems, and that will negatively impact productivity.

5. "You might share things you shouldn't." It's too tempting to unload work issues or gripe about other employees to your employee friends.

6. "It's not fair." You might find it difficult to separate personal feelings from professional feelings when you're making employment-related decisions.

7. "It's hard to fire a friend." That sums it up in a nutshell.

On its face, each point Tabaka raises is true. It *is* hard for a leader to be friends with employees. It isn't always easy for employees to be friends with each other either. Employees get promoted, and suddenly a peer is now a leader. *Awkward* (insert high-pitched teenager's voice).

I, too, believed each of Tabaka's seven principles before I made a decision based on new information. Before I started my business, I spent more than a decade as a lawyer, focusing on employment law and litigation. My job was to give clients advice on how to minimize their risk. In that life, I consistently advised my clients to keep their personal and professional lives separate.

If a leader didn't have a clear head and couldn't make unbiased employment decisions, I feared the company would be at risk. I envisioned a flood of lawsuits, each one costing companies a minimum of six figures (factor in attorneys' fees, settlement costs, lost productivity due to time spent in depositions and hearings and trials, and it adds up quickly). Leaders would be distracted, and the distraction would become another cost, perhaps tens of thousands of dollars in lost business time.

But I was wrong. I was so wrong.

I learned how wrong I was when I was serving as associate general counsel at The Hershey Company. I no longer was giving legal advice in a vacuum without relating that advice to the faces of real people who would feel its impact.

I learned that each and every decision involved *people*, and we can't make decisions based on statistics or probabilities or trends alone. We must consider the human factor.

When people are losing jobs because of a lack of work, for example, we need to remember that they are going home and telling their families that the paychecks will be stopping. As a consultant, I have urged clients to have compassion when laying off employees around holidays. We need to make tough business decisions, but we can do it with heart.

For example, I was working with John (true story, but not his real name), a senior executive of a company that had recently been acquired. He was explaining how hard it was for him, even after thirty years in business, to lay off an employee. He said that, even with his years in business, it still kept him up at night. But he explained, "I would be more worried if it didn't keep me up at night. The day I stop caring about the people is the day I need to stop what I'm doing, because this company is nothing without its people."

In his book, *Big Potential*, happiness researcher Shawn Achor encourages us to change how we think about success and what we do to achieve it. He studied 1,600 students to identify the individual attributes that correlated most directly with the potential for success. To his surprise, the best indicator of success was not a student's SAT score or personal wealth or the number of friends one had on Facebook. In fact, test scores and money and other things did not correlate *at all* to success. One factor alone was the standout: social connection.

Strong social connections, Achor explains, meant lower rates of depression, higher rates of optimism, and an overall healthier state of well-being. Social connections also correlated directly to professional success once the students left college. Achor calls it the "survival of the best fit," meaning those with strong relationships had higher rates of long-term professional success than their isolated counterparts.

Based on his 1943 paper entitled, "A Theory of Human Motivation," and the subsequent 1954 book entitled, *Motivation and Personality*, Abraham Maslow would agree. Maslow set forth his famous hierarchy of needs, often explained with the pyramid, with the most fundamental needs at the bottom and the self-actualization we experience at the top because of the needs being met:

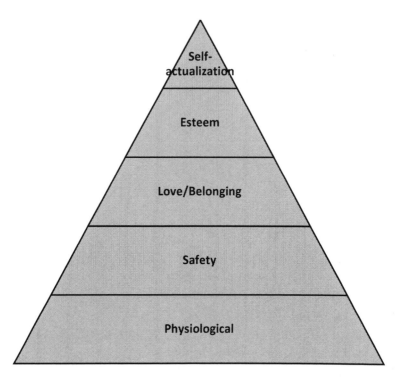

Physiological needs are the most basic needs we have for survival: air, food, water, and sleep. Safety refers to our need to feel safe and secure in our environment. In the middle of the pyramid is our need to feel like we are part of a family, a community, a team. Esteem represents our need to be recognized and rewarded for our efforts, and self-actualization is our need to do our best at whatever we do. Each level of the hierarchy applies to our personal lives as equally as it applies to our work lives.

Corporate America has done a great job at offering snacks and even nap rooms to their employees. They regularly express their commitment to providing a safe place to work. They've spent a ton of time and money on employee rewards and recognition programs, and they rely on each individual's desire to do their best to propel the business forward.

In doing so, however, Corporate America has skipped over the middle – the heart of the pyramid. They have failed to remember that what comes before and what comes after, above and below, are meaningless if we don't have the sense of belonging and community – the *relationships* to our co-workers. Without the relationship, there is no fulfillment. Without fulfillment, there is no desire. Without desire, there is no commitment.

Frientorship puts love and belonging – the *heart* – back into the pyramid. Frientorship puts people first. When we do that, everything else falls into place.

To avoid building connections with the people in your organization – your team, your co-workers – is a gross miscalculation of the realities of the workforce, and it places an insurmountable burden and limitation on success. If I had the wherewithal and business acumen (and the benefit of Achor's books) as an attorney to conduct a proper risk-reward analysis, I would have realized that my legal advice was saving the company in the short term, but crippling it in the long term. Besides, great leaders can have relationships with their teams *and* make the necessary decisions for the business.

As in our personal lives, so much of the day-to-day work we do involves some kind of emotion, whether it's anger, frustration, joy, excitement, enthusiasm, or anything else on the emotional spectrum. It's no wonder the relationships we have with our co-workers and our leaders have such a big impact on us and our potential for success. With so many variables in business, how we connect with each other as human beings is the one constant always within our control.

Yet how much time do we spend fostering relationships? How much time do we spend developing our *heart* as part of our professional development? Not much.

Instead, we spend countless hours in continuing education courses to maintain our certifications. We spend countless hours at industry conferences learning the latest trends. We spend countless hours schmoozing at networking events. Comparatively speaking, however, we spend very little time nurturing the people – the heart of any organization and the one thing a company has that gives it a true, competitive advantage in the marketplace.

I was delivering a frientorship workshop for a client recently. Fifteen of the engineering company's up-and-coming leaders were seated around the conference room table. Some were local. Others came from satellite offices. Some had been with the company for over ten years. One had been with the company for six months. We began with introductions and a couple of simple questions:

1. What brought you to this company? Some of their answers:

    •   I was frustrated by poor leadership at my former company. Leadership didn't even know who I really was. I heard great things about the people and the culture here.

    •   This company is heavily invested in making people happy.

- I started here as an intern. I really liked it here, so I ended up staying.

- I came here for my boss.

- This company made me promises, and it kept all of them. I love the culture here.

- I can't work in a place that doesn't care about me.

2. What keeps you here? Some of their answers:

   - I want to make sure everyone feels invested in the company and that people are getting the attention they need from their supervisors.

   - I'm here because I enjoy the people I work with.

   - I like the people.

   - I'm in awe of my boss.

   - This company cares.

This company gets it. Each answer has one thing in common: the *relationship* employees have with each other and with their leaders. I cannot think of a single workshop participant or individual I coached who said the money and perks alone were what kept them from leaving and going somewhere else.

While money might draw someone to a company, it goes only so far. The financial honeymoon period ends quickly. Employees realize they want more than money. Employees want frientorship.

FRIENTORSHIP FACTS

- ◆ The days of coming to work, punching in, doing a job and going home – with little connectivity – are gone.

- ◆ Historical and modern research proves that great relationships and a sense of connectivity are key indicators of professional success.

- ◆ Perks might attract people to your company, but they won't keep them there.

CHAPTER 3

SETTING THE MINDSET

Mind is a flexible mirror, adjust it, to see a better world.

~ Amit Ray, *Mindfulness: Living in the Moment – Living in the Breath*

During my workshops, I always pause at the end of the introduction, hoping the cynics in the room will identify themselves. When they do, they usually say things like, "I understand what you're saying, but I work hard to keep my personal life separate. I don't want to go out for beers on the weekends with my employees or co-workers. I want to go out with my friends."

And then there are the organizations whose leaders say, "I'm not hiring people to be friends at work. I'm not hiring them to go out to lunch and have fun together. I'm hiring them to get a job done for me. If they don't like it, they can go work somewhere else." I get it. The reason the company exists in the first place is to deliver a product or service. Leaders want to make money. They want business to succeed. They want shareholders to be happy. It's understandable.

One day I received a call from Jane (real call, but Jane was not her name). Jane was planning a conference for an association made up of manufacturing companies, and she was looking for a keynote speaker. I told her about frientorship and what I cover in a typical keynote and how I tailor each message to make it relevant to the day-to-day working lives of the audience.

Jane really liked the program messages. She was concerned, however, that the topic would be too "soft" for the association members. I understand. I worked with manufacturing clients for years as an attorney. I stood beside hourly employees on the manufacturing lines, I spent countless hours in the C-suite and I nervously presented to the corporate directors. I understood the concern.

This concern, though, is misplaced. It reflects a certain perspective, reflective of a mindset focused on seeing things only one way instead of realizing the potential, both professionally and economically, of envisioning something in a new or different way. When we approach things with tunnel vision, we tend to think there is only one way of doing something, and we struggle to find that one way to make sure we don't make a mistake.

Jane, for example, feared selecting the wrong speaker. She didn't want to alienate herself from the association members, possibly putting her job in jeopardy.

But there is no single, correct way of doing just about anything. There are usually several. One way, of course, is to approach it as Jane and the leaders described chose to do so. Another way, though, is to expand your mindset and open yourself up to the possibility that there is a *better* way – a way to accomplish what leaders and employees both need and want in order to deliver the best business results while still driving profits. We do that by turning things on their heads (at least from the old perspective) and focusing on building great relationships inside the workplace.

Being willing to recognize the impact that workplace relationships have on individual and organizational success depends on your mindset. Stanford University psychologist Carol Dweck conducted numerous studies which reveal the stark contrasts between a fixed mindset and a growth mindset and the potential for achievement with each.

People with a fixed mindset see only one way of doing something or believe that they are born with the talent they have and that's the end of it. When facing a difficult challenge, for example, students with fixed mindsets were likely to quit or, even worse, cheat. An organization with a fixed mindset sees only one way of doing something. Failure to comply means there isn't room for you in that organization. You are easily replaceable and anything but indispensable or a valuable resource.

People with a growth mindset, however, don't see themselves as being "born with it." An individual with a growth mindset is hungry for learning new and different things, seeks continuous improvement and knows there isn't only one way of doing something. The students Dweck studied went from having some of the lowest test scores to the highest test scores over the course of one year when they believed they had the potential to learn more. They rose to the challenge. An organization with a growth mindset sees disruption or headwinds as opportunities. They see their people are ripe for development and see the potential for talent to be harnessed. The leaders see it, too, and they plan for succession to ensure business continuity, work hard to develop and retain their teams, and consider them part of a family or community where relationships matter.

That's where frientorship comes into the picture.

A growth mindset is ripe for devouring what frientorship has to offer. The first step is realizing that not every workplace relationship fits neatly into a single mold. The focus is on making sure we have each other's backs and are lifting others up to achieve goals together rather than stepping on them and clawing their eyes out so that we can achieve our individual career goals. We start by opening our minds to the possibility that maybe we've been going about our individual work and performance one way for a long time, and this one way is neither the only way nor the best way.

If we reexamine how we treat our co-workers and our teams and how we connect with them, how would we grade ourselves on a scale of one to ten (one being the lowest and ten being the highest)? How would we rate ourselves in a performance review if one of the questions were, "How did I treat my team, my co-workers, my assistant this year?"

If the answer is that you didn't focus on that or never thought about it before, or don't consider it relevant, then the frientorship method is exactly what you need to help reshape your mindset. (And incidentally, if that question isn't part of your performance review process, it should be). Frientorship gives you the tools to see the potential in yourself as well as others, and to rethink how you will define and achieve success, both individually and for the organization you serve.

FRIENTORSHIP FACTS

- The idea that building strong workplace relationships matters is not fluff. It is necessary for success.

- When learning something new, you must have an open mind and recognize that potential is limitless.

- Before moving on to the next chapters, reflect on how you have approached workplace relationships. Have you made this a priority?

CHAPTER 4

SMASHING THE FRIENDSHIP STEREOTYPES

Piglet sidled up to Pooh from behind.
"Pooh!" he whispered.
"Yes, Piglet?"
"Nothing," said Piglet, taking Pooh's paw. "I just
wanted to be sure of you."

~ A.A. Milne, *The House at Pooh Corner*

Muhammed Ali said, "Friendship is the hardest thing in the world to explain. It's not something you learn in school. But if you haven't learned the meaning of friendship, you really haven't learned anything."

When we think of friendship, we tend to think of the relationships we have to a close group of people with whom we spend our time when we are *not* at work.

Merriam Webster defines friendship as "the state of being friends." "Friend" is defined as "one attached to another by affection or esteem." It's about a connection, a personal connection we feel for another person. Friendships can come and go based on life circumstances. For example, I have a handful of friends from what I consider to be the various stages of my life: early education and high school, college, golf, law school, legal jobs, entrepreneurship, my neighborhood, parents of my kids' friends, etc. Each person plays a role in my life, and each relationship is purposeful and meaningful.

Our friends are the people we call when we have a crisis, when something amazing happens to us, when we want a book recommendation, when our marriages are falling apart, or when we want to go to happy hour... you name it. If there is a life event, we are sharing it with our friends. If that is the only way we view friendship, though, then we have tunnel vision, a fixed mindset.

Friendship comes in a variety of forms, and the depths of friendship are varied. As described, I have different friends who serve different purposes in my life. Some of my closest friends are from jobs I've had over the years. Immediately prior to starting my own business, I was working at The Hershey Company. I had a special group of work friends who made being at work everyday *fun*. We laughed, commiserated, supported, celebrated, cried, and yelled. Lauren, Jen, and Lois – otherwise known as my Chocolate Posse – were my collective safety net.

Importantly, my Chocolate Posse relationship was built on three foundational elements: trust, loyalty, and respect. That foundation empowered and required us to be brutally honest with each other, not telling each other what we wanted to hear, but rather what we needed to hear. It meant that I could be vulnerable, and they would not turn around and use my vulnerabilities against me. It fostered collaboration rather than competition among us, and enabled us to build each other up, even when the chips seemed to be down all around us.

I had been at Hershey about three months when a serious employment matter arose. My boss, the general counsel, had a conflict, meaning she was not able to provide counsel to the corporate directors. I found myself – the newbie on the block in the legal department of a then-$6.5 billion company – guiding a discussion in the boardroom with the likes of former Homeland Security Secretary and Governor of Pennsylvania Tom Ridge and other bigwigs from corporations around the world.

To say I was nervous would be a huge understatement. The day of the big meeting, I went to my Chocolate Posse. I told them I was a wreck and that I'd spent most of the morning in the bathroom with an upset stomach. Naturally, they laughed at me. But after the laughter ceased, they reminded me that I was prepared and knowledgeable and that the people sitting around the boardroom table were human beings, not monsters.

Was I still nervous? Yes. But I knew I had a few people rooting for me. And I knew they wouldn't take my insecurity and turn it into a reason to belittle or shame me.

At work, relationships are set up much like the structure of the organizational chart:

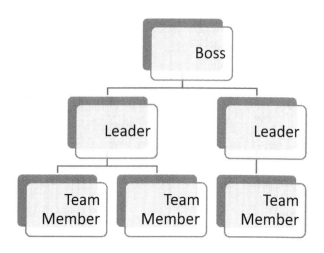

We have vertical relationships in the form of supervisor-subordinate and horizontal relationships in the form of peer-to-peer. Each of the forms is critical for organizational success, but each has different boundaries and expectations.

As Patricia Sias[5] explains in "Narratives of workplace friendship deterioration":

> Friendships are unique workplace relationships in two ways:
>
> (1) friendships are voluntary – although individuals do not typically choose with whom they work, they do choose which of those individuals to befriend.
>
> (2) friendships have a personalistic focus in which individuals come to know and treat each other as whole persons, rather than simply workplace role occupants.

---

[5] Patricia Sias, "Narratives of workplace friendship deterioration," *Journal of Social and Personal Relationships*, 2005, Vol. 21(3), pp. 321-340.

It's about more than clocking in, doing a job, and clocking out. It's about understanding who someone is, what interests they have, where they live, what their family is like, what they do in their free time, and so on. Sias explains further that workplace friendships serve as "the source of emotional and instrumental support."

Add to the workplace relationship dynamic the age, race, religion, gender, and other differences, especially today when millennials will make up 70 percent of the workforce by 2020 and we are working in the era of #metoo and #timesup.

I'm often reminded of the line from one of my favorite movies of all time, *When Harry Met Sally*. Billy Crystal and Meg Ryan play college classmates brought together by a mutual friend to share a cross-country car ride. The overarching question through the entire movie is, "Can men and women ever be *just friends*, or will sex always get in the way?" Not only can they be *just* friends, they need to be.

Yes. Sexual tension exists in traditional male-female relationships. According to Camille Chatterjee's article in *Psychology Today* entitled "Can Men and Women Be Friends," the belief that it's impossible stems from decades-old stereotypes of men working while women did not work outside of the home. Men and women have been working together for years now. As with any working relationship, they need to define the parameters of the relationship and work within those boundaries.

With millennials tearing down the walls of gender stereotypes more than ever, there is no excuse for failing to build productive relationships regardless of gender. One of the great benefits of these friendships is the ability to garner perspective from someone who isn't the same as we are. The same holds true for other multi-cultural relationships. We broaden our perspectives, we increase our awareness, we become more inclusive, and we break down barriers that once kept us socially siloed.

Contemporary politics have become increasingly divisive, leading to everything from arguments to fist fights at work. Some companies are employing five generations of workers. We are bombarded by stereotypes of people based on their age. Millennials are entitled and lazy. Boomers have no understanding of technology and no desire to learn it. Gen Xers are overlooked and stuck between two worlds, unsure of which one they want to inhabit. Society is becoming more diverse. We need to stop thinking in terms of stereotypes and start fostering discussion and dialogue at work to get to know each other's strengths and interests. We have far more in common than we think.

Upon joining a law firm as a partner, my welcome was mixed, perhaps as mixed as the firm was at the time. The more seasoned partners were excited and welcoming. The millennial associates were all over the place in terms of reception, from ecstatic and warm to less-than-enthused and cold. One associate, Amanda (her name is real and used with permission), was a bit chilly.

Amanda is one of those super smart people. She graduated from high school early, then graduated from college in three years and completed her joint Juris Doctor and MBA degrees in four years. She was what we called a "homegrown" attorney at the firm, working as an associate there ever since law school graduation three years prior. She was a no-nonsense woman.

And here I was, the attorney who'd made a lateral move from one firm to another and entered the firm as a partner. From my perspective, I had a good book of business to bring to a law firm (meaning I had enough paying clients to cover my expenses and be profitable), so I tried to negotiate a great deal for myself, which is exactly what we all should do. To Amanda, I was an unknown variable.

I decided the best way to get to know her was to work with her. I started bringing her in on my projects a little at a time. After that she started coming to me with projects and marketing ideas. It became apparent very quickly that she was smart and business-savvy. She was a hard worker. She was responsive. She was great with my clients. Did she have a bit of an edge? Yes. But so did I, and there was so much more to her than the edge.

As Amanda and I worked together more and more, her initial dislike of me – the outsider – waned. The more she learned about me, the more she believed that I deserved my place in the firm. I had a great practice. I knew what I was doing. I knew how to develop relationships with my clients. I was legitimate. And I knew she was, too.

Amanda-the-Millennial and Claudia-the-GenXer became not only close colleagues, we became close friends. She had a lot of ambition, and was very vocal about it. That kind of drive can be off-putting. I spent so much time with Amanda, though, that I understood what made her tick. Could she be overly-ambitious at times? Sure. Could she be hard on people? Yes. So could I. No one is perfect.

I'd rather work with someone who is overly-ambitious than someone who has no vision. Besides, her ambition was contagious, at least for me. I figured if she was going to push the envelope, I needed to work that much harder for what I wanted. I did not see her as a threat. I appreciated what I could learn from her just as much as she appreciated what she could learn from me. It took time to get there, but our friendship has survived job moves and moves to different states and a barrage of networking groups and all of the ups and downs of life.

It would have been so easy for me to write Amanda off the minute I met her. After all, I was the new kid, and (at least in my own mind) it was she who rejected me at first. I could have labeled her an entitled millennial or rejected her ambition or attitude. Instead, I chose to get to know her by working *with* her instead of against her.

I learned later from Amanda that she had mentors encouraging her behind the scenes to work with me as well. By working together, we delivered great results for our clients. She connected me to other people who became great friends and clients. We trusted each other, we were loyal to each other, and we respected each other, even when we didn't necessarily agree with each other. We built a great *friendship*, and our friendship enabled us to generate revenue as colleagues in a law practice. It was a win-win. Even though we don't work together anymore, we're still winning.

Building great workplace friendships extends beyond the confines of the four walls of a business. Think about all of the service-based industries, such as legal, accounting, banking, real estate, wealth management and so on. The one thing keeping a client from switching to another service provider is the relationship the client has with the business, and that relationship usually boils down to a single individual. Some people call them relationship managers. When they do it well, I call them friends.

We've all seen the television ads for the wealth management company where the financial advisor calls his client to see how the college visits with the client's son are going and to offer savings strategies to help pay tuition. The message from the company to the audience is, "We *know* you. We *care* about you. You are *not* the same as every other client." It's personal. It's based on building a meaningful connection. That connection – that *friendship* – is what keeps us from switching relationships with our service providers whenever a new provider wines and dines us for our business.

Speaking of wealth management, I met a guy recently who works in that business. We'll call him Mark. We met at a party at a mutual friend's house. We decided to meet for lunch to learn more about each other's work. I've since had lunch with Mark four or five times. Not once has he made a sales pitch to me to become my financial advisor. Not once has he asked me if I have any friends I can refer to him. He *has* asked me about the work I do, who my ideal client is, and how he can help me. He wanted to learn about me, to help *me*. In doing so, he formed a professional friendship with me. In turn, my family has formed a personal friendship with his family. He wants to help me be successful, and I, in turn, want to help *him* be successful. That's what building social connection through professional conversation can do. And it just so happens that he's a man, and I'm a woman, and we are just friends.

FRIENTORSHIP FACTS

♦ Great workplace friends do not use your vulnerabilities against you. They have your back.

♦ If we take the time to build friendships with the people at work who do not look like us (gender, age, race, ethnicity, disability, etc.), we can build inclusive workplaces.

♦ Great relationships increase both employee and customer satisfaction and retention.

CHAPTER 5

BUILDING IMPACTFUL WORKPLACE RELATIONSHIPS

I think if I've learned anything about friendship, it's to hang in, stay connected, fight for them, and let them fight for you. Don't walk away, don't be distracted, don't be too busy or tired, don't take them for granted. Friends are part of the glue that holds life and faith together. Powerful stuff.

~ Jon Katz

The Gallup Organization routinely polls employees, asking whether they have a best friend at work. Gallup asks the question because they know it matters.

Employees with close friendships at work have a more positive view overall of company culture. When employees have close work friendships, their companies get a more creative environment, more teamwork and collaboration, shared knowledge, and knowledge transfer. Customer satisfaction is higher. Employee retention is higher.

All of these things add up to greater job satisfaction and more happiness and, consequently, higher employee engagement. Engagement breeds success. It isn't the other way around.

It's easy to attract people to a great place to work. Engaged, happy employees are the best advertisement a business can have, especially in the era of social media and glassdoor.com. Just ask Yelp, who managed a media firestorm after two employees decided to blog about their employment experiences and got fired for doing so. Yes; there are always two sides to every story. Today, however, the employer's side of the story is more likely to lose the public relations battle.

Employees at all levels, from entry to CEO, need great workplace friendships. They need someone to tell them when they have been too hard on a team member in a meeting, or to challenge them to look at something a little differently. That's what work friends do. In other words, we all need someone to save us from ourselves, because we're human, and we're going to make mistakes. It's okay to make those mistakes, provided we are willing to accept feedback and change our behavior.

We know workplace friendships have a powerful impact on engagement, productivity, company brand, and ultimately, profits. Why aren't more companies focusing on these friendships?

Some leaders feel it's outside the scope of their responsibilities. As I explained in Chapter 3, some leaders don't want their employees to be friends, despite the plethora of science and data that points to the benefits. Some simply don't know where to begin to cultivate workplace friendships. The good news is that it is not difficult.

Workplace friendships are something we build. It's one cup of coffee at a time. It doesn't take a huge amount of time, and the little moments add up. If you're in an office building, you're walking by offices or cubicles every single day. Stop and pay attention. Look at the photos and items your colleagues choose to have around them at work. We tend to put things on and around our work areas that are meaningful and important to us. If folks work remotely, don't underestimate the value of chit-chat at the beginning of a telephone or video call.

There are dozens of electronic collaboration tools on the market to help us build connections and stay connected at a time when we are more disconnected than ever. *PC Magazine* rated the best online collaboration tools and apps for 2018 that they say will reduce time spent on e-mail and allow for more time to get work done while building connectivity. Slack, Zoho Projects, LiquidPlanner, Volerro, Airtable, LeanKit, and Podio are only a few examples. A simple Google search will reveal their precise strengths. Everyone wants us to work smarter these days. "Work smarter, not harder," they say. We can do that, but that doesn't mean working alone. We must continue to work together.

A group of high school students know and understand what Corporate America seems to have forgotten. They know that isolation and loneliness combine to create unhappiness, resulting in students being unengaged and apathetic at school. They know that teen suicide rates are at a thirty-year high. They decided to take matters into their own hands by forming an organization called, "We Dine Together (WDT)" (for more information, visit www.wedinetogether.org). Their mission statement says it all:

> Uniting & empowering individuals to create inclusive environments through the belief that long-lasting relationships are built over the table.

WDT is a student-led organization that focuses on ensuring new students integrate into their new environment. They provide a safe-haven for students who are feeling alienated, lonely, or ostracized. The concept started with one simple idea: no student should ever eat lunch alone. The WDT members actively seek out isolated students, sit with them, eat with them, get to know them, and show them that they aren't alone. Importantly, WDT believes that these small acts of inclusion are teaching students about friendship, and in doing so, building tomorrow's leaders. It's a simple concept. It's brilliant. And a group of kids did this.

As Murthy warns of the workplace loneliness epidemic occurring in adults over the age of forty-five, the WDT model is ripe for replication at the corporate level. It speaks to a crucial point in the employee life cycle: onboarding. If a group of high school students can ensure that new students integrate into their new school community without having a budget or a way to spend a lot of money, then Corporate America surely can ensure that new employees integrate into their new work environment.

Acme Company (name changed, but the story is true), a long-time client of mine, used a great onboarding software program that sent e-mail reminders to both the new employee and the employee's manager. The e-mails supplied hyperlinks to the new-employee paperwork that needed to be completed and submitted. Everything had a deadline. If the employee missed a deadline, the manager received an e-mail alert. The alert was supposed to ensure the manager would follow up with the employee and – you know – *manage* the employee properly. The onboarding system provided a smooth process that reduced hands-on time for completing paperwork and made the jobs of human resources and the manager a lot easier.

The problem, however, is that the software had the unintended effect of reducing manager interaction with the new employee when it was supposed to increase it. Managers ignored the e-mail alerts in overwhelming fashion. An e-mail search revealed in one circumstance that the manager deleted the vast majority of these e-mail alerts without ever opening them. Additionally, communication between manager and new employee came to a screeching halt.

Technology helps, but it does not and cannot replace the obligation of a manager to spend time with a new employee, to build a relationship with a new employee, and to help the new employee build relationships with other team members.

Leaders need to use the technology the way it is meant to be used, as a trigger for dialogue. That is far more important overall for the business than delivering an electronic handbook that will never be read by anyone other than the lawyers.

The best thing about building connectivity to foster relationships is that it comes with little to no cost to the company. Think of how many days you spend eating your lunch alone in your office because you're "so busy." Think how many of your team members eat lunch alone in their offices to try to prove to you that they're working really hard. As my friend and coach, John Dame, has said on many occasions, we wear "busy" like a badge of honor. At what cost?

If you take two days a week and change "eating alone" to "eating together," the connections will start to build over time. People will learn more about each other. They will find common ground, and they will appreciate differences, just as I learned to understand what made Amanda tick. Lunch doesn't have to be a two-hour excursion. It can be a quick, twenty minutes. It doesn't have to involve going out to a restaurant. It can be "brown bag day" once a month or once every other week. Again, the little moments build big connections.

If you still feel like you don't have time, then think about how much meeting time is wasted by accomplishing nothing. I'm willing to bet that you spend time in meetings going around the table and having everyone report on what they're working on that week or that month. It's a complete waste of everyone's time and fosters an environment where people try to show they are busier than their colleagues.

Instead, start the meeting by going around the table and have each person share a victory – something he or she accomplished personally or professionally since the last meeting. It sets a tone for success, and it gives insight into the person's character and priorities. Doing so brings people closer, enabling them to work together to achieve more and more success.

Move on to having the team discuss one or two major objectives and what they need from their peers to be successful. Everything else that is for informational purposes only can be sent via a memorandum to read outside of crucial meeting time.

Perhaps one of the easiest things a leader can do is walk the halls and say hello. I can't tell you how many times I've spoken to employees at different companies who said, "They [the leaders] walk right by us as if we don't exist."

I had the privilege of attending a memorial service for a CEO who passed away unexpectedly. The room was packed with employees wearing the organization's signature color. The CEO was known and celebrated for how he knew the names of almost, if not all, 1,000+ employees. I learned at his memorial that he used to walk the halls in his building and greet every employee from center cubicle to corner office with a smile and a hello. He made them feel valued and appreciated just by saying hello and knowing their name.

Being able to greet your team by name is one of the simplest ways to show them you care.

FRIENTORSHIP FACTS

◆ Connecting in small ways over a period of time can build strong and meaningful workplace friendships.

◆ Stop wasting time in meetings. Celebrate victories and use the time to collaborate for greater successes.

◆ Know your team members and co-workers by name. A simple "Hello, Joe," shows you care, which motivates and inspires top performance.

CHAPTER 6

MENTORING: BE TRADITIONAL NO MORE

If you want a harvest in one year, grow a crop. If you want a harvest in ten years, grow trees. If you want a harvest that will last a lifetime, grow people.

~ Chinese Proverb

What is mentorship? It's a relationship we have with a trusted counselor, advisor, or teacher. Mentors don't tell us what to do; rather, they help us understand different circumstances and make informed decisions. They ask us a lot of questions. They offer us their experience in situations with which we are unfamiliar or don't have as much experience. Mentors do not consider our inexperience to be a negative mark on our résumés. They see our desire to learn as the ultimate plus.

I've had many mentors over the course of my life and career, and I continue to work with several on a regular basis. Too many to name. Many of my mentors remain friends to this day. Some were friends first but turned into mentors. When I started my consulting business, for example, I didn't know the first thing about how to register a domain name or design a logo or build a website or design business cards (and the list goes on and on and on). That's where my friend, Kim, came to the rescue.

Kim spent hours with me. She made a checklist of things I needed to do to set up my business. Kim had owned her own business for nearly fifteen years before I started The Human Zone. We had been friends for over ten years before we found ourselves sitting in a hotel room trying to brainstorm names for my business, and she's been by my side on this entrepreneurial journey ever since.

A couple of years into my business, a friend contacted me. She was about to start her own consulting business after years of practicing law and working as a Human Resources professional (sounds familiar, right?). She needed some advice about how to start her business. I knew it was my turn to send the checklist and answer questions, and I didn't bat an eyelash. That's what you do. But not every mentorship starts out like these.

Meet June (at some point or another, we all have been June). June was really excited to start her first day in the marketing department for XYZ Corporation. XYZ really had their act together when it came to onboarding her, she thought. June started receiving e-mails on her personal e-mail address as soon as she accepted her offer. She filled out all her paperwork electronically and submitted it before her first day of work (the former lawyer in me will ignore whether this constitutes compensable time under the Fair Labor Standards Act). She completed the required post-offer, pre-employment drug test. On day one of her new job, she was ready to go!

June spent half of her first day in a training room learning the history of the company and key information about XYZ's operations and benefit plans. After that, June's human resources business partner (HRBP) met with her to give her a little bit more information. The best part, the HRBP explained, was that XYZ matched her with a mentor, Sally. Sally was the most senior employee (in terms of years of experience) in June's department. Sally would be able to show June the ropes. They had lunch once in June's first week of work, and that sums up the entire nature of that mentorship.

The human resources function at Jane's company experienced a lot of change in the last ten years. Through no fault of their own, they found themselves having to justify their value to the companies they served. It's part of the pain of being a cost center in an organization rather than a revenue generator. In their effort to prove their worth to business leaders, many human resources professionals began designing and implementing processes to find, attract, and develop the best talent and, once hired, to differentiate performance among talent. The result for some mentorships meant that a process was established in many organizations whereby a senior employee would be paired with a new employee and BOOM – a match made in heaven was born. For about five minutes.

On its face, a match between a junior and senior employee is not a bad idea. In fact, research reveals that typical mentors are defined as:

> Individuals with advanced experience and knowledge who are committed to providing support for the purpose of increasing career advancement of junior organizational members or their protégés.
>
> ~ Gosh & Reio, "Career benefits associated with mentoring for mentors: A meta analysis," *Journal of Vocational Behavior*, April 2013

The problem is that tenure-based relationships focus myopically on career advancement. "Career advancement" might be the big-picture goal, but it isn't specific enough to be meaningful on a day-to-day basis. Plus, such mentorships are usually random, and random mentor-mentee pairings do not ensure that the mentor is equipped to meet the needs of the mentee.

In most cases, random, tenure-based matches are based solely or primarily on years of service. Pairings based on tenure have little to offer either the mentor or the mentee, as we saw with June and Sally. Mentors in these circumstances also tend to shape the mentee's perceptions of other co-workers by delving into the mentor's beliefs about office politics. This can be helpful in some cases, but it can also backfire and end up unfairly poisoning the mentee's perceptions. It is not a guaranteed recipe for success.

Should companies have formal mentor programs? Only if they go about it purposefully. Mentoring is meaningless if it isn't purposeful. Instead of matching random people based on age and/or seniority, companies need to understand what skills their employees need to develop, and they need to commit to helping employees develop these skills. This is the part of the process where human resources partners can be extremely valuable. If both the HR partner and the leader (or just the leader if your company doesn't have an HR function) have a short discussion with the employee, mentoring for success can take flight.

It goes something like this:

> Leader: June, I'm really excited to have you on our team. As you begin your work here, I want you to think about where you want to go with your career. It's my job to help you succeed. If I do that, I know this company will succeed.
>
> [Picture June's beaming face as she explains how she wants to be the next CEO of the company.]
>
> Leader: Great! Now for the hard work. You need to think about your skills. What do you do really well? Where do you need help developing? Write it down. Then I'd like you to meet with our HR partner, Mike. Our HR team knows the people in this organization inside and out. Mike will help you find people here who excel at what you need to develop. It will be your responsibility to reach out to them and ask for their help. Understand the rules, though: (1) You must be respectful of their time; (2) You must take responsibility for your professional development; (3) The world is bigger than this company, so don't forget to look externally for help that you can apply internally.

The key is individual ownership of this process. Employees must have a stake in their own professional development; otherwise, they will be victims, blaming their employer for not doing enough *for* them. It is our individual responsibility to know what we know and know what we don't know and to find the people who can help us fill our gaps.

Our career development is just that – *ours*. I'm not sure at what point we started believing that it was our employer's responsibility to take charge of it, but that's wrong.

Should the employer make every effort to stay in tune with our development and support us on our journey? Yes. They have resources that can support our efforts, and they have contacts and connections that can supplement what we are able to do on our own. Leaders who don't have their fingers on the pulse of their team members' career aspirations don't retain great people. In the end, though, it's up to us. We need to stop waiting for someone to do something *for* us. We need to do it ourselves. Seek it out. It is exponentially more fulfilling on both a personal and professional level when we chart our own development course.

When considering who makes a great mentor, break out of the mold of looking only at people more senior than you in a department or company. People at all levels in an organization can be mentors. Organizational rank might not have anything to do with life experiences or strengths. Look horizontally and vertically. Look past age. Again, age does not necessarily equate with a specific strength of experience. Boomers can learn from millennials just as much as millennials can learn from boomers. Look beyond the physical attributes that make us different from each other.

I had a chance to attend Gair Maxwell's *Branding Highway Boot Camp*. Gair is a branding expert and TEC Canada's Speaker of the Year. We hit it off instantly, perhaps because his dad was born just a few minutes from the first tee at St. Andrews historic golf course in Scotland. Gair is a great speaker with a great message on how to rethink your company's branding strategy. I was even luckier to be able to have dinner with him. As we connected, I learned that one of Gair's most influential mentors is nineteen years old, and the mentorship began when his mentor was just seventeen.

Gair, a Gen Xer, routinely seeks counsel and advice from his stepson, a member of Generation Z. It all started one day when the young man showed him a video of a YouTube star. Gair dismissed it at first, but then realized his stepson was showing him the future of marketing. Gair had the perfect resource to learn the latest technologies and keep his finger on the pulse of how up-and-coming generations will filter information to make consumer decisions. Brilliant.

Leaders know that diversity drives business results, but most companies struggle to build diverse cultures. Mentoring can change that. When seeking out mentors, look for people who look different from you. Build diversity by getting to know someone of another gender, race, national origin, etc., while simultaneously building your skillset. Drive diversity within your company and within your life organically, one mentorship at a time. Doing so will strengthen the diversity within a company. It will also go a step further by fostering inclusion through connections.

Importantly, pay special attention to the plural – *mentors*. No one person holds the key to our professional development. We need multiple people from multiple backgrounds with different skillsets to develop ourselves more completely.

Can you have a bestie? Of course, but don't lose sight of the end game. It's not only good for your professional development, but it's also good for building your network and teeing yourself up for another opportunity in case the marriage to your current employer ends in divorce.

Thanks to technology, we have more opportunities than ever to find mentors and to be mentors. Social media sites such as LinkedIn are ripe for great professional relationships, provided you connect with people in a purposeful way. I've seen it go south quickly, and it usually looks something like this:

> Jeff: Hi, John. I see that you wrote a book about how to build a great résumé. Attached is a copy of mine. Would you please take a look and tell me what you think?

> John: Jeff, I'd be happy to work with you. I charge a flat fee of $1,000 to review and edit a résumé. Thank you for your interest.

Jeff is annoyed that his request for some quick help is being met with a four-figure fee rather than a simple, "Looks good" or "Perhaps rework section two" response. Jeff then starts telling his network that John is selfish and greedy, and we've got an old-fashioned-modern-day bashing underway.

Jeff needs to remember that John provides a service for a fee. There is a huge difference between asking someone to work for free and asking someone if he is willing to form a relationship that can be mutually-beneficial.

Here are a few simple rules for seeking mentorships with strangers:

1. Have a plan. Identify the frequency (how often) and duration (how long will each session last) of meetings or discussions with your mentor. Identify how you will connect (via telephone, videoconference, e-mail, in person, a combination). Be sure to specify your need and why you selected this individual to help you with that need. Offer references for your character and commitment.

2. Remember that mentoring is a two-way street. Never ask for help without offering help in return. This is accomplished with a single statement at the end of any mentor request: "Likewise, please let me know if there's anything I can do to assist you with your [business, career, network, etc.]."

3. Do not ask someone to work for free. Finding a mentor does not mean you are asking someone who works as a professional development coach to coach you for free. If that's your goal, you will never reach it. Instead, you can reach out and let the coach know that you would like to improve your communication skills, for example, and ask the coach if he or she can recommend any resources that might be helpful (books, TED talks, people).

4. Be respectful of our most valuable resource – our *time*. People are busy. Do not expect them to give up hours and hours of time each month to help you. It is

not realistic. Communicate clearly in your request for help that you understand how valuable the mentor's time is, and you do not want to waste it or use it unnecessarily.

5. Mentorships, like any relationship, are a commitment. Don't make a commitment you can't keep. Remember that the mentee is the one asking for help. That means the mentee is the one responsible for driving the relationship. A mentor is not going to hound a mentee to stay committed to the relationship. A mentee who demonstrates commitment, though, is an individual to whom it's worth committing.

Here's a sample outline you can use to track progress and share with your mentor as your relationship progresses:

Development Areas:

☐ [Insert two to three skills to develop.]

Deliverables:

☐ [Identify expected outcomes.]

Timeline:

☐ [Build a reasonable timeline for execution.]

Tools and Resources:

☐ [Identify sources of support and learning, such as books or book chapters, TED talks, conferences, classes, or courses that will supplement individual coaching.]

Noticeably absent from the rules are references to online safety. It should go without saying that safety comes first, and you should avoid connecting with strangers without vetting them. The moment something seems off, end the mentorship and take all necessary steps to block and report inappropriate contact. Been there. Done that.

FRIENTORSHIP FACTS

♦ Mentorship is a relationship built on trust and respect with an advisor, counselor, and coach.

♦ It is our responsibility to take charge of our career development. Mentorship is a way to both foster meaningful connections and increase our skills.

♦ Mentorships are two-way streets. Always be willing to offer to help your mentor. Chances are, you have strengths that can benefit your mentor.

CHAPTER 7

THE BENEFITS OF GREAT MENTORSHIPS

Tell me and I forget. Teach me and I may remember.
Involve me and I learn.

~ Benjamin Franklin

The first and most obvious benefit of mentorship is that we develop skills that we once lacked. There are so many benefits to mentorship that go beyond skill development for mentees, and those benefits extend to mentors, employers, customers, and clients.

A lot of companies are very good at attracting great people. They can tell a wonderful story and have rockstar employees participate in the recruiting process and paint an overall picture of a company that would make anyone want to get on that train. Many companies fall short when it comes to retention, though. It's almost as if they check the box when they fill a vacancy and move on to the next one without putting substantial effort into retention.

Employee turnover comes with a high cost to the company, bringing with it both direct and indirect costs.

The obvious ones are the dollars that follow an employee out the door. Those costs include advertising, time spent by employees reviewing résumés and conducting interviews, travel costs for applicants, hiring bonuses, relocation costs, training costs, uniforms, drug testing and other post-offer, pre-employment screenings. It adds up quickly.

Then there's the work that isn't getting done by the employee who walked out the door. "Oh we don't have that problem," says XYZ Corporation, "because we take that work and spread it around to the other employees in the department until the vacancy is filled." That might work for a week or two or maybe even a month, but chances are the vacancies aren't filled that quickly. Employees who are already at capacity because of their own jobs are now being asked to take on more work (without more pay, by the way). Any way you slice it, work is not getting done. When work isn't getting done, a client or customer's needs are not being met. Period.

The other hidden costs associated with high turnover include lost productivity because of time spent complaining by employees who are picking up the slack. You might not be able to measure employee frustration on a day-to-day basis, but those costs add up, and their frustration is legitimate. High turnover has a direct impact on morale. Morale has a direct impact on productivity.

Sometimes an emergency arises, and it's understandable. It is important to ensure that the emergency is just that – an emergency, an exception, not the norm. When turnover is high, though, great performers tend to be rewarded with more work to keep up with demand. Adding work to an already-overloaded plate on a regular basis is not a win for the employee, and promising to remember the hard work done in January and February when it's time to do performance evaluations in December is akin to Wimpy offering to pay me Tuesday for a hamburger today.

Studies conducted by the Society for Human Resources Management (SHRM) inform us that the cost of replacing a salaried employee is approximately six to nine months of that person's salary. Take Joe, a manager earning $50,000 per year, for example. Joe quits. His company is going to spend about $38,000 trying to replace him by the time you factor in recruiting and training costs. Those dollars are specific to Joe's job and do not reflect the indirect costs we already discussed.

A 2012 study by the Center for American Progress (CAP) demonstrates the high costs of turnover with even more specificity (see chart on next page) Note that top executives can cost dramatically more to replace than even the annual salary figure. If you have a highly-educated employee earning $100,000 per year, you are looking at spending $213,000 to replace her. The perspective that everyone is replaceable is fine, as long as you have an endless supply of money.

The industries with the highest rates of voluntary exits from their jobs[6] are leisure, hospitality, and food and beverage, with construction and transportation running closely behind.

Mentoring, when done correctly, reduces turnover and increases retention. In doing so, it reduces money flying

---

[6] Boushey & Glynn, "There Are Significant Business Costs to Replacing Employees," Center for American Progress, Nov. 2012.

out the window and increases the bottom line for employers.

Position	Cost of Turnover
Jobs that require specific skills (other than executives and physicians)	21% of salary
Workers earning less than $75,000 annually (which covers 90% of all U.S. workers)	20% of salary
Workers earning $50,000 annually or less (which includes 75% of U.S. workers)	20% of salary
Workers earning $30,000 annually or less (more than 50% of U.S. workers)	16% of salary
High-paid executives and highly-educated positions	213% of salary (that is *not* a typo)

Source: Boushey & Glynn. "There Are Significant Business Costs to Replacing Employees," Center for American Progress, Nov. 2012.

Mentoring also increases employee engagement. Companies with successful mentoring programs are reducing silos and helping to foster meaningful relationships. Employees are less likely to be tempted by a few more dollars when they have something more important than money – *meaning*.

Additionally, great mentorships (similar to great workplace friendships) help companies ensure knowledge transfer in key positions. If a key position becomes vacant without warning or the ability to plan, employees don't have to struggle to get up to speed on historical matters of significance. There are few things worse for a client than trying to find someone at a company who knows and understands their history with their vendor. An absence of that understanding sends the unintended message that the relationship isn't important. If a client has to start from scratch with someone, the client can just as easily start from scratch with a competitor.

Mentees in successful mentorships report success with professional development and a better understanding of the company culture. These results are obvious for internal mentorships. It is important to have someone you trust, to whom you can go with a question or by whom you can run something to test your perspective on a situation.

Mentees perform their jobs better, because they are receiving real-time feedback and incorporate that feedback immediately. Great mentors also are imparting leadership wisdom on their mentees. Whether the mentor is internal or external, the mentee is absorbing unspoken leadership characteristics that are crucial for individual and organizational success. Mentors bring active listening, problem solving, and coaching to life each time they work through an issue with a mentee. For internal mentorships, the game of office politics becomes a lot less complicated.

WHAT'S IN IT FOR THE MENTOR?

Researchers have long studied the benefits of mentoring on mentees. The benefits for mentors are often overlooked but are critically important, especially if we are encouraging people to take time away from their already-jam-packed days to be of service to another *for free.*

Mentors also develop critical skills through mentorship. They are tasked with having tough conversations with their mentees, which means they are practicing and learning how to give difficult feedback and have conversations that aren't always the pat-on-the-back we all want. In doing so, their leadership skills improve, and it positions them to succeed when forced to have similar conversations with direct reports, either presently if they lead a team or down the road when they do.

Mentees are uniquely situated to bolster the reputation of their mentors, both publicly and internally. Branding is a huge part of any success equation. Mentees help mentors appreciate different perspectives, particularly if the mentorship involves individuals from different genders, generations, ethnicity, etc.

The ability to see things more broadly is also a critical leadership skill. Mentors develop professionally while they're helping someone else develop. It's a win-win relationship and, therefore, not a waste of anyone's time.

Perhaps most importantly to the individuals involved, mentorships result in higher compensation for both mentors and mentees over the course of their careers, perhaps $30,000 or more annually. This isn't pocket change. This is real money. If that isn't motivation enough to find a great mentorship, I don't know what is.

FRIENTORSHIP FACTS

- Both mentors and mentees develop professionally with a great mentor relationship.

- Great mentorships reduce turnover, increase engagement, increase customer satisfaction and drive profitability.

- Great mentors become great leaders, and their mentees are the ultimate brand ambassadors of their abilities.

CHAPTER 8

THREE THINGS YOU MUST HAVE TO LEAD

"It is a curious thing, Harry, but perhaps those who are best suited to power are those who have never sought it. Those who, like you, have leadership thrust upon them, and take up the mantle because they must, and find to their own surprise that they wear it well."

~ J.K. Rowling, *Harry Potter and the Deathly Hallows*

First and foremost, it is essential to understand that leadership is not reserved for CEOs. Leadership is not reserved for the *boss*. We all are leaders at every stage of our career journeys, whether we are leading ourselves or a team of thousands. We all have the power to influence others to do great things, and we must use that power to bring out the greatness in ourselves and others.

I am the youngest of four daughters. My traditional, Italian-American father's dream of having a son was dashed when the doctor exclaimed, "Well, Frank, four of a kind beats a full house!"

Not long after I was born, my dad nicknamed me Clyde. He was a huge fan of Clint Eastwood. In the movie *Every*

Which Way But Loose, Eastwood played a trucker who had a pet orangutan named Clyde. That's right. My dad nicknamed me after an orangutan.

As soon as I could walk and talk, he started taking me fishing with him. We spent days fishing for rainbow trout in upstate New York, and I developed a love and appreciation for nature. But it's what he introduced me to when I was ten years old that would turn out to be the most impactful and important leadership lesson of my life.

Because I'm the youngest, my dad was able to spend time with me that he didn't have an opportunity to spend with my older sisters. He had taken up the sport of golf in his thirties and had significantly more time to play as I was nearing ten years old. One day, he asked me if I wanted to come to the golf course with him and ride around in the golf cart.

At ten years old, I didn't exactly have a rockin' social life. "Sure," I said.

We had a great day, and I enjoyed riding around in the cart. Besides, when you're a kid hanging around with a bunch of old people (at ten years old, everyone over twenty is "old"), you're the most popular person around. The attention was great.

The next time my dad was heading to the course, he dangled another carrot. "Would you like to come to the golf course with me again tomorrow? You can drive the cart around for me."

A ten-year-old *driving* something? *This is awesome*, I thought. After our usual Sunday morning attendance at

7:45 A.M. Mass, I went to the golf course with my dad, and I drove the cart around the course like a champ.

The next time I went to the course (because, after all, I'm the official golf cart driver now), I stood on the green with my dad, who was facing the menacing three-foot putt for par. "Would you like to putt this for me," he asked.

I had played miniature golf dozens of times. *How hard could it be?* "Okay," I said.

I missed, but my dad didn't care, and neither did I. "Try again," he said, "and keep putting until you knock it in."

I knocked it in... eventually.

The next time I went to the course (because, after all, I'm the official golf cart driver *and* pinch putter, if you will), I stood next to my dad as he prepared to chip the ball on to the green. "Do you want to chip this one up onto the green for me? Try to get it as close to the hole as you can."

Okay, I thought. *This looks easy.* And so I chipped the ball onto the green *and* I got my dad's putter and putted the ball into the hole.

Then it happened. We got up on Sunday, went to 7:45 A.M. Mass and headed to the course again. This time, though, my dad asked me if I wanted to take his club and take a full swing at the ball and see what happens.

Yes! Yes. I wanted to go for it. I had been watching my dad for weeks, and he had given me small tastes of this big game. Now I was ready for the whole thing.

I accepted his 7-iron, took a full swing, and whacked the ball. "Wow. You're a natural, Clyde," he exclaimed with joy.

I fell in love with golf at ten years old. The following summer, I found myself competing in my first tournament. I loved it that much.

Years later, I would find myself capitalizing on a partial golf scholarship and playing competitively in the Big 10 at Penn State. Years after that, golf made almost every job interview I had a piece of cake. The men interviewing me for legal jobs wanted to talk about golf, my handicap, how often I played, what my favorite course was, and – most importantly – how well I could perform in a scramble tournament. As a lawyer, I was the token golfer for most client tournaments, because I could play from the red tees and give the men a chance to hit the par five greens in two shots. Win, win, win.

The ultimate lesson – the one I would come to piece together decades after I first rode in that cart with my dad – was leadership. My dad hadn't looked at me and said, "You are coming to the golf course with me today, and you are going to learn how to play golf." He didn't take me with him on that first day and hand me a golf club and tell me to start hitting the ball. He didn't sign me up for a tournament before I had ever touched a club. That would have been a disaster. Instead, he gradually introduced me to something new and taught me little by little how to do it until I was ready to go all out, all by myself.

Great leaders take their teams on a development journey. They don't put someone in a job they've never done before and just expect them to know how to do it.

It's remarkable how many times a leader hires "top talent" or promotes "top talent" and then considers that person a failure because she doesn't instantly understand every single aspect of the role. The leader is essentially handing the person a golf club and telling her to take a swing, rather than giving her exposure and a few lessons along the way so that she can be ready to take the reins and build on existing successes.

LEADERS VS. MANAGERS

There are so many books and articles and TED talks and materials out there on leadership. We know there is a huge difference between being a leader and being a manager.

Managers maintain the day-to-day, the status quo. They make sure the task at hand gets done. They watch over things like attendance. They track production numbers. They are not thinking about the business much beyond the end of that day or the end of the week.

Leaders, however, are focused on the future. Leaders commit to ensuring the job gets done while thinking of new and better ways to do it, and who the people are who will follow in their footsteps. Leaders are working to develop and empower their teams to be prepared to take the golf club and whack the ball when it's their turn.

At the end of the day, great leaders must have three critical attributes so they are able to take their teams on the right development and empowerment journey: a high level of self-awareness, the ability to hold themselves and others accountable, and excellent communication (verbal and written) skills. Without these three attributes, leaders are destined for mediocrity or, even worse, failure. Their failure is a failure to the people they have been entrusted to lead and a failure to the businesses they are obligated to propel to success.

1. SELF-AWARENESS

My family adopted a rescue dog in August of 2016. Her name is Katy, and she's a combination of German Shephard and Australian Cattle Dog. My daughter, Marena, was twelve years old when we adopted Katy. That pre-teen face resembles a disgruntled employee from time to time! Anyway, Katy was really strong. Her predator instinct made her even stronger. It took every ounce of strength I had to hold on to the leash when a brave squirrel or rabbit would cross our path.

Marena asked me when she would be able to walk Katy by herself. I replied, "Maybe in a couple of years when you're a little older and a little stronger, and she's a little older and a little less strong."

I could see the wheels spinning in Marena's head as she turned and said, "But by then I will be fourteen or fifteen. Isn't that the time when I will be so wrapped up in myself that I'm not gonna want to do things like take the dog for a walk or hang out with you?"

After I stopped laughing, I replied, "Well, honey, if you know yourself, and you want to avoid becoming that kid, then it shouldn't be that difficult. It's called self-awareness, in a pre-teen sort of way."

Simply put, self-awareness is our understanding of what makes us tick and why we think, feel, act, and react the way we do. It's an understanding that every thought and feeling we have came from somewhere along our life journey – we learned it from something or someone – and that is what makes us who we are. Self-awareness is the most important skill for anyone who wants to influence others, because it is what makes us genuine and authentic.

A high level of self-awareness gives you the ability to "ch-ch-chickety check yourself, before you wreck yourself," as Ice Cube would say. The great thing about self-awareness is that it is something upon which we can improve and build no matter how old we are or at what stage we find ourselves in our career. Of course, we need to have the right mindset to be willing to learn (see Chapter 3). Assuming you do, there is no stopping your ability to increase your level of self-awareness.

Self-awareness is an essential foundation for building trust, which is an essential element of building workplace friendships and mentorships.

Self-awareness is also the first step toward goal-setting, because it enables employees to identify strengths and weaknesses, which in turn enables employees to harness strengths appropriately and develop weaknesses without being derailed or distracted by them. Sometimes what people think they can do (or what they think they're doing) is vastly different than their actual ability or contribution. That doesn't make them bad people; it means they lack a high level of self-awareness.

Not every person is meant for every position. High self-awareness enables people to level set their own expectations.

You might know someone like Bob. Bob (real guy, but name changed to protect privacy) was a phenomenal sales employee promoted to a leadership position.

This is a common scenario. We take the best employee and promote them to a leadership role without teaching the best *employee* to be a great *leader* who can help others be great at *their* jobs. Bob went from being the best sales person to being the manager of a large sales team.

Upon promoting Bob to the leadership role, his boss asked me to help Bob grow into the new role as a leader. As part of the leadership development process, I administered a 360° review. A 360° review is an electronic survey I send to the client, the client's boss, peers, direct reports, and any other individuals who work regularly and directly with my client. Each person rates my client on a series of leadership characteristics. We compare my client's self-review to the others' reviews. Assuming respondents provide truthful answers, we are able to gain insight into whether my client's perception of his performance as a leader is aligned with the perception of his boss and others.

When I studied the results of the 360° review, I learned that Bob rated himself substantially higher than his boss and peers in a couple of key leadership skills: "listens to others" and "communicates effectively."

I asked Bob to focus on those two elements in conjunction with the written comments. What did he think of that? "That's wrong," he said. "I've gotten really good with communication."

That's what I call the "perception gap." The perception gap is the space between what we think of ourselves and what others think of us. It helps determine our level of self-awareness. If the gap is big, our self-awareness is low. If the gap is small, our self-awareness is high. In Bob's case, the perception gap for communication was big.

Bob certainly isn't the first leader to have a high perception gap in certain areas. The key question in a circumstance like Bob's is whether Bob is willing to reflect, accept the feedback, and take the steps necessary to improve communication skills. If the answer is yes, the possibilities are endless. If the answer is no, someone like Bob does not have a long-term future as a leader. Sooner or later, a perception gap that goes uncorrected will catch up with you.

2. ACCOUNTABILITY

When leaders have a high level of self-awareness, they can hold themselves and those around them accountable. Accountability is a round-the-clock obligation – one that starts in childhood and never ends. Being accountable means we are defining and accepting the consequences for our own behavior and ensuring we hold our teams responsible for theirs.

One day, I was going through my daughter Carissa's school papers. She was in fourth grade at the time. I came across a math test and noticed something that vaguely resembled my husband Steve's signature. I showed the paper to Steve and asked him if he had signed it. Nope. "Well, you should talk to her about it, because she forged *your* signature."

From my perspective, I was off the parenting hook for this one. A couple of hours later, I asked Carissa if her dad talked to her about the math test. "Yes," she said. "He told me that I committed a crime, and I shouldn't tell anybody, because I could go to jail."

Did I mention my husband is a lawyer? He just lawyered up our nine-year-old kid.

"No," I said. "You *will* go to school tomorrow, and you *will* tell your teacher what you did, and you *will* accept the consequences. You have to be accountable for the choices you make."

I ran into her teacher a couple of weeks later, and I asked him if Carissa had spoken to him. She had.

"She told me she 'forgitated' her dad's signature, and that he told her she shouldn't say anything because she could go to jail. But her mom told her she had to tell me because she had to be accountable."

I take the wins wherever I can find them.

Accountability isn't just for when people get caught making mistakes, though. It's equally as important to ensure we recognize and celebrate the wins.

Accountability also isn't just for when there's a tangible consequence, such as a lost client or a lost profit. Hurt feelings matter and can set a team up for failure if not properly addressed. Carissa wasn't going to jail, but she was going to learn what it felt like to have a tough conversation and to admit to someone that she lied.

One of the greatest accountability failures in the workplace occurs when leaders hold employees to different standards. Employees who carry their weight and behave appropriately lose respect for leaders who let co-workers slide. When they lose respect, they lose their will to put in the extra, discretionary effort it takes to do the job well. And the zombie starts to creep in, and they don't do anything more than the minimum to get the job done. The minimum isn't good enough anymore.

The lack of accountability most often happens with behavior, not productivity. Leaders have no problem telling employees when they failed to meet their production quota or some other, tangible deliverable. They struggle, though, when it comes to addressing behaviors. It's the difference between saying, "the only thing that matters is what you do," and "what matters is not only *what* you do; it's also *how* you do it."

The stories are common and were plastered all over the news in the last quarter of 2017. High-powered producers such as Harvey Weinstein and Matt Lauer had the best kept secrets of alleged and admitted bad behavior in their respective industries. Their boards and bosses explained they had no idea what the men had done. Many in the court of public opinion, however, believed leadership knew and chose not to hold the men accountable to clearly-defined standards of behavior because of the potential loss of profits. Only the people involved know what happened, but it's a cautionary tale for all businesses in all industries.

The world is changing, and with that change comes instant and powerful demands from clients and customers and sponsors to ensure those who behave badly are held accountable for their behavior. While these examples may seem extreme, similar things are happening in businesses all over the country and the world. In general, high performers who behave badly are given more chances than poor performers who behave badly. This does not incentivize performance. It decreases morale, which results in an increase in employee absenteeism and a lack of desire to perform.

In many ways, employees are like children. Children thrive in environments where the consequences for behaviors are clearly defined and routinely enforced. Employees thrive, and therefore perform, at their peak in environments where they are held accountable for their behavior, not only their production of widgets.

3. COMMUNICATION

Communication is what transforms someone from an authoritarian – a boss – into a leader. A great leader communicates goals. If you're aiming for nothing, that is exactly what you will hit every single time. An expectation that isn't effectively communicated to the people expected to fulfill it is nothing more than meaningless words, and will result only in frustration for the leader and those who desperately are trying to please that leader.

Perhaps the single greatest workplace communication failure comes in the form of the annual performance review. Nothing should ever come as a surprise. I learned this principle as a little kid. My first performance review came in the form of a single question: "Have you been naughty or nice?" The answer would determine whether Santa would bring me coal or presents.

Can you imagine if my parents didn't shape my behavior over the course of a year and then coal appeared in my stocking? Yet that's exactly what happens every single day at work. The difference is that we are talking about raises, bonuses, promotions, and even job security instead of Christmas presents.

If you've ever sat in a performance review taking a hit and thought, "Why is this the first time I'm hearing this?" then you know what I mean. If you have ever provided year-end feedback to an employee who asked why she had not heard what she was doing wrong until that moment, then you need to improve your communication and learn to point out the hits and the misses in a more timely fashion.

It begs the question: are you living the definition of insanity? Are you doing the same thing year after year but expecting different results?

We set year-long goals, we don't check in regularly (with ourselves, with our boss, with our teams) to measure our progress against those goals, and we get sidetracked by the unexpected emergencies that pop up along the way. Come year end, we find ourselves scrambling to do as much as we can to meet the goals we set, but ignored, several months ago.

Stop the insanity with a few, simple steps to better goal setting and goal *achieving*:

♦ Set goals correctly. Good performance goals are specific, timely, relevant, and objectively measurable. Leaders must review goals set by employees and provide feedback as early in the goal-setting process as possible. This enables leaders and their teams to have clear expectations about the critical work to be done over the course of the year.

♦ Identify the things you must do over ninety-day periods of time to achieve your goals. Great goals give everyone the big picture of what must be accomplished over the year. Without breaking them down into smaller chunks of work, you have the perfect recipe for procrastination and cramming at the end of the year. Instead, identify the specific actions you must take over the next 90 days (and then the next, and so on) to stay on track to deliver the big picture. Not only does this help you prioritize your work, it's the perfect setup for one-on-one meetings with your boss or team members to review progress and stay on track (*see* next step).

♦ Be flexible. Stuff happens. It could be anything from a natural disaster to an acquisition, to a supply chain failure and everything in between. Just because you have a goal, it doesn't mean it has to be the *only* goal. As situations arise, revisit your goals to make sure they still make sense. Adjust as necessary, but be sure to go back to the previous steps each time you need to adjust your goals.

♦ Take the initiative to check in with your boss to discuss your progress against goals. If you're the boss, you should be engaging in regular and timely coaching so that both you and your team member know exactly where everything and everyone stands. Great goals and 90-day execution plans provide the perfect backdrop for every leader-employee meeting.

♦ Celebrate the wins along the way. As my dad used to say during a round of golf after I hit a bad shot,

"There are no pictures on the scorecard. Get the job done." Not everything will be done perfectly. Celebrating includes the ability to recover after a mistake or unexpected headwind gets you off track. It makes the big victories that much sweeter.

Stick to this plan, and you will find yourself working in a collaborative environment where expectations are clearly defined and understood, team members are highly engaged, goals are being met or exceeded, and business is thriving.

BEYOND PERFORMANCE MANAGEMENT

Performance management is only one piece of workplace communication. Amy's (fake name, real situation) company was beginning a project to restructure and reorganize certain functions. The planning stages for the restructure were, at that time, the company's worst kept secret. Rumors began swirling early and often, but discussion was taboo. As a leader herself, Amy had a team of three people who were in tune with the rumors. She wanted to be able to anticipate and address any questions or concerns they would have as the company moved forward.

Amy sat in a leadership team meeting and asked, "What do I tell my team if they ask me what will happen to their jobs? They are going to want to know what this means for them."

"Just tell them the company might look different, but the work still will need to be done," replied one senior leader.

"But that doesn't address their concern, which is a legitimate one," Amy replied.

The senior leader brushed her question off, leaving Amy to wonder if she had overstepped her bounds not only by asking, but also by pressing for a better answer.

In Amy's case, she needed to "tow the company line." Amy knew that towing the company line here would kill trust and respect. At the same time, some information needs to be confidential, and there's a fine line that every leader must walk between confidentiality and transparency.

Employees are smart, and they can spot a company line a mile away. In asking Amy to deliver the company line, the senior leader purposefully or inadvertently chipped away at her team's trust of Amy, and in turn, Amy's respect for the company.

Perhaps it would have been better for Amy to tell her team she understood their concern, but unfortunately, she was not sure what the structure of the department would be when the project was complete. Amy would do her best to keep her team informed as the process unfolded.

This situation is common. Leaders intentionally or unintentionally fail to communicate with their teams in a way that responds to their needs. When we are underinformed, we tend to assume the worst. Employees want real, truthful answers to questions. Leaders increase employee loyalty and increase employee commitment by being transparent and honest.

FRIENTORSHIP FACTS

- Without high self-awareness, the only person we can lead is ourselves. The success rate of even that is extremely low.

- Leaders who do not hold team members accountable to the same standards of production and behavior will not generate long-term success.

- Transparent communication is what transforms one from a boss into a leader.

CHAPTER 9

HOW TO BE GREAT

To handle yourself, use your head; to handle others, use your heart.

~ Eleanor Roosevelt

You know the skills you need to have to be a great leader. You know that you're a leader regardless of what your job title says. Every person is in a position of influence.

The question then is, how do you go from being the person you are now to the leader you want and need to be? How can you be better, whether it's for yourself on your career journey, for your family, for a team of ten you manage, or a team of 1,000 you someday want to manage?

The great news is that it doesn't have to be hard. There are changes you can make that can have the dramatic ripple effect of a tiny pebble tossed into a large pond.

INCREASING SELF-AWARENESS

Raising self-awareness starts with asking yourself one question: who am I? In asking who you are, what you really want to know is, "What's my story?" Your story matters. It is why you are who you are.

Think back to being as young as you can remember. Going forward from there, build a timeline of the defining moments in your life: the good, the bad, and the ugly. What happened? How did those events shape you? As you think back on them now, do you feel the same today as you did in the moment? Why or why not? How did those events make you the person you are today?

YOU'RE NEVER TOO OLD TO LEARN

When I was in third grade, my father experienced a trauma that would define him for decades to come. He owned his own pharmacy in the heart of downtown Utica, New York, called Oneida Square Pharmacy.

In those days, the pharmacy was open until 10:00 P.M. One evening, minutes before closing, two men walked into the pharmacy, and a nightmare unfolded. The men pulled a gun on my dad and proceeded to sweep the drug shelves and the cash register clean. Next, they demanded that he open the safe and give them whatever cash was in there. Peering around the corner in the back office, one of the robbers saw a stairway and asked my dad where it led.

"That's the basement," he answered.

"Go down the stairs," they ordered. As he put his foot on the first step, he flipped the switch to turn the lights on in the basement. "Turn that off," they ordered.

He walked down the stairs in the dark to the unfinished, damp basement, followed by the two robbers with the barrel of a gun poking into his back. When he got to the bottom and turned the corner, the robbers barked out another order. "Get down on your knees and close your eyes."

He felt the gun pushing into the back of his head. *This is it,* my dad thought. *They are going to kill me.*

"Start counting, and don't come up those stairs until you get to one hundred," they directed.

He counted to one hundred. Five times. Then he slowly went upstairs, went to the phone, and called the police.

He was fine, physically at least. That night would turn out to be a defining moment in my dad's life, and it would later become a defining, educational moment in my own. Neither I nor my dad would understand that, though, until decades later when he was in his early seventies and I my thirties.

You see, the two robbers were African-American men, and for the years that followed that night, my dad would attribute the bad acts of two men to an entire class of people. I was not allowed to sleep over at my African-American girlfriend's house in high school, and my dad didn't want her sleeping over at our house. He never articulated why, and he never made a racist comment in my presence. He certainly never thought of himself as a *racist.*

Decades later when we were discussing the robbery, he told me that he didn't realize what he had done, but that, in hindsight, he knew. He knew he was wrong. And he was so glad that we did not take his trauma and make it our own and grow up feeling the same way he had felt all those years.

He came to that realization in his seventies. It's never too late to understand why you think, feel, and act the way you do. Once you understand why you are the way you are, you are empowered to change.

MANAGING EMOTIONS

I learned over the course of my twenties that I have a hot temper. I can go from zero to 60 faster than a cheetah. Sound familiar?

Whether it's a tendency to overreact, bark out orders or completely shut down when being challenged, knowing and understanding your tendency is half the battle. It takes time and effort, but you can improve. For me, I learned to recognize when my blood was starting to boil. A deep breath and a little time can go a long way.

It's funny how whatever made me want to lash into someone on Monday didn't seem like such a big deal on Tuesday. Stop. *Feel* the reaction. Don't respond. Give it at least a couple of hours. I'm still not perfect, but I have a better ability today to understand my triggers than I did ten years ago.

Your response after the simple passage of time will be less (fill in the blank – heated, emotional, personal – you name it), and it will be more thoughtful and deliberate. You can deliver a tough message without being caustic. You can teach your body not to shut down in the face of adversity. When you understand yourself, there is no limit on what you can teach yourself to do.

I remember sitting in a performance review when I was an attorney, and I knew I was hearing feedback on things for the first time. I knew my boss had not discussed the pain points with me prior to that review. In that moment, I wanted to scream. I wanted to fight back. I wanted to cry. I paused and said, "I think I hear what you are saying. If it's okay, I'd like to think about it and come back to meet with you either later today or tomorrow." No problem, my boss said. Had I not left when I did, I would have responded emotionally. I needed time and space to gather my thoughts and respond factually.

It is a great strategy to ask for time to think about what was said before you respond. It shows you are listening and trying to be purposeful. Are there situations where you absolutely *have to* think on your feet? Yes. Of course. You need to be able to think on your feet. You also need to recognize situations where you can and should ask for time to respond. Use that time to calm your emotions and develop your facts.

TOOLS AND RESOURCES FOR DEVELOPING SELF-AWARENESS

As kids, your parents and teachers tell you to treat others the way you want to be treated. It's the Golden Rule. Forget it. You need to treat others the way *they* want to be treated. That's the Platinum Rule. We all are different, and others' needs might not be the same as ours.

There are a few hacks that great leaders can use to help build the self-awareness they need to abide by the platinum rule. First, pick an assessment out there on the market. Use that assessment, and be completely truthful when you answer it. You can use the DiSC® Profile, Kolbe assessments, StrengthsFinder, the Color Code, or another survey designed to increase self-awareness and build emotional intelligence.

Use the assessment to learn who you are, how you tend to react, and what dominant personality traits you possess. Do not, however, use the assessment as an excuse or justification for bad leadership.

Just because you are a high "D" (meaning direct) on the DiSC® profile does not vindicate you from telling everyone exactly what you're thinking all the time. It means you need to understand who is comfortable with hearing things directly and for whom you might need to soften your tone to best make a point.

Another option is a 360° review, as discussed in Chapter 8. In most 360° reviews, you are scoring yourself (and others are scoring you) on a number of different leadership qualities. Your perception will be compared to the perception of your boss and others. It gives you an opportunity to see where you are aligned and where your self-perception is way out of whack with how others perceive you to be doing your job as a leader.

A 360° review, however, is only as good as the truthfulness of the answers. Be clear to those you're asking to participate that you want their open and honest feedback so you can grow as a leader and a person.

When you get feedback you don't like or that catches you off guard, do not try to figure out who gave it. Do not track people down and ask them why they answered the way they did. I appreciate how difficult it can be to resist the urge to figure out who said what, but that is not the point of a 360° review.

I've seen leaders go on the hunt. Doing so destroys workplace relationships. When done correctly, however, the review builds trust and loyalty, the foundations of excellent workplace relationships.

Instead of hunting the naysayers down, let everyone who participated know you received their feedback and will be working hard to improve certain areas. Let them know you'd be open to a discussion with anyone who is interested so you can develop an even better understanding of feedback they provided. Identify an accountability partner who can help keep you on track and provide important, real-time feedback to you on your improvement journey.

ACCOUNTABILITY IN ACTION

It is difficult to hold others accountable for meeting expectations if we are incapable of holding ourselves accountable for our own mistakes. With a high level of self-awareness comes the credibility we need to be the coach of our teams. If we are coaching regularly, the traditional performance review process becomes less necessary. In fact, one of the best things a company can do is *stop conducting annual performance reviews* and instead develop great coaching cultures.

Ten years ago, as an attorney representing big business for all labor and employment-related matters, I would have doubled over and clenched my chest at the thought of giving up annual performance reviews. Maybe my advice was part of a problem rather than a solution.

Annual performance reviews create the documentation upon which attorneys can rely when defending (or, when they're poorly written, pursuing) employment litigation matters. The best leaders are coaching their team's performance on a regular basis and documenting their conversations to ensure understanding, thereby making an annual performance review a formality and, consequently, a waste of time.

Leaders who coach rather than manage have regular and timely meetings with their employees to review what is working and what is not, providing guidance to harness the employee's strengths while improving upon weaknesses and mistakes.

Leaders with high levels of self-awareness who coach their employees send the message that failure *is* an option. Coaching involves not only drawing upon what you learned from your successes, but also drawing upon your own mistakes, sharing them with your team and reminding them that perfection is unwanted and, ultimately, impossible.

SAY 'I'M SORRY,' AND SOUND LIKE YOU MEAN IT

Perhaps the single greatest example of imperfection comes in the form of an apology. If you're saying you're sorry the right way, you're admitting that you could have done something better. It doesn't necessarily mean you were *wrong*. It means there was something that could have been done *better*.

A great apology does not offer excuses disguised as explanations. A great apology does not sound like the title of Demi Lovato's hit, "Sorry Not Sorry."

There is a huge difference, for example, between saying, "I'm sorry you feel that way," and, "I'm sorry I made you feel that way." Mathematically, we are talking about saying two more words. Emotionally, we are talking about making something worse versus acknowledging and moving on from the mistake.

It is not about being right or wrong. You might disagree one hundred percent with whatever it is you are being accused of doing, but starting with, "I'm sorry I made you feel that way," does not admit wrongdoing. It sends a signal that you agree the person feels a certain way and that you did something (right or wrong) to cause it. From there, you can move forward.

EFFECTIVE ELECTRONIC COMMUNICATION METHODOLOGY

The way we communicate can make or break an apology or any other message we attempt to convey. George Bernard Shaw said, "The single biggest problem in communication is the illusion that it has taken place." Over ninety percent of how we interpret a message comes from the body language and tone of the person conveying the message. This is scary when you think about how many messages you send via e-mail or text. We hide behind screens to avoid having tough conversations face-to-face, but doing so only makes matters worse.

Understanding we live in a digital era, we can be smarter about how we communicate electronically, both as senders and receivers of messages. For senders, there are a few simple rules that can guide any electronic message you craft:

1. Understand what you're trying to say. Sounds simple enough, but it runs deeper. You need to understand if you're writing to inform, educate, make a request, or for generic informational purposes only.

2. Know your audience. If the purpose of your message is to educate, for example, are you writing it to someone who knows more or less than you about the subject? You do not need to prove how smart you are to your boss or your subordinates. Just tell them what they need to know in as few words as possible.

3. Take a step back after the message is written and re-read it. Consider how it might be perceived by the recipient. What tones will she infer? Your intent is only a piece of the message puzzle. The recipient's perception and inferences matter, so try to understand and adjust for them before you hit the send button.

4. If you need something from the recipient, ask for it up front. Do you need an urgent response? Make sure you say that first or, better yet, put "URGENT – RESPONSE REQUESTED" in the subject line of the email. When the subject lines convey what the recipient needs to do, it makes filtering through a stack of emails after a long day much easier, and it guarantees a response to your request in a timely manner. "FYI ONLY" tells me I can read it Saturday morning instead of at 11:00 P.M. Wednesday night when I'd rather be climbing into bed.

5. Avoid sending negative feedback via e-mail or text at all costs. An urgent response is one thing, but I'm talking life or death urgent. Speak in person when you must deliver bad news or difficult feedback. Pick up the phone if you can't do it in person because of time zones or travel schedules. Have the difficult conversation with

spoken words so that a tough situation isn't complicated by negative inferences.

Recipients have a few hacks to make electronic communications less stressful for them as well:

1. Assume positive intent. We already know how hard it is to get the intended tone of a message without seeing and hearing the sender deliver it. So why do we jump to the worst possible conclusion when we read a message? Stop it. Just stop. Assume the sender is coming from a good place, and you will immediately infer a better tone in the message.

2. Seek to understand. If you assume positive intent and it doesn't take you to a better place, resist the urge to respond with rage. Instead, respond with a few questions. Saying, "I want to make sure I understand and that I'm not reading anything into your message. If I understand you correctly, you would like (fill in the blank). Can you please let me know if I'm on the right track?" Most of the time, a softer response begets you, in turn, a softer reply. It's also a great way to deescalate a bubbling situation.

3. Stop replying to everyone on the message. Senders make mistakes all the time. In an effort to cover their own behinds, they send a message to fifteen people when there might be only five who really need to get it. Don't be a copycat. Look at the original recipient list when replying and determine who needs to read your response. And for heaven's sake, the only person who needs to

get a "thank you" message is the original sender of whatever made you feel grateful.

4. Just because someone sent you an e-mail or text does not mean you have to reply with written words. You have the choice to pick up the phone or walk down the hall to the person's office to further discuss a matter or seek the clarification you need to understand the message. People may claim it is easier to whip off an e-mail. It is not easier on anyone. It is a copout when a better alternative is staring you in the face.

Both senders and recipients tend to use written words as a way to cover their behinds, but it turns into an excuse to avoid having the difficult conversations in person. Instead, send an e-mail after a tough discussion to summarize the outcomes and action items of that discussion. That is a perfect use of electronic communication and ensures commitment to the path forward. When in doubt, try your hardest to convey information rather than emotion.

FRIENTORSHIP FACTS

♦ Develop a higher level of self-awareness by asking for, being open to, and responding to feedback from multiple sources.

♦ If you coach your employees regularly, the annual performance review becomes a non-issue for everyone.

♦ Streamline electronic communications to give recipients what they need and to reduce the daily barrage of e-mails and text messages.

CHAPTER 10

PUTTING IT ALL TOGETHER

Don't follow the crowd. Let the crowd follow you.

~ Margaret Thatcher

Combining the principles of friendship, mentorship, and leadership is about more than adding one to another and another. It is about the purposeful intersection of the three concepts. The following diagram best illustrates this point:

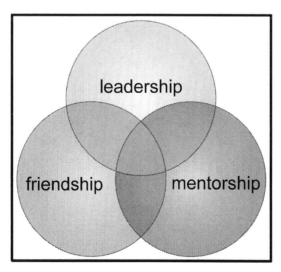

Trust, loyalty, and respect – the key elements of friendship – are also the foundational elements of a mentorship and crucial components of a relationship a leader has with a team. A mentor is a trusted advisor, counselor, and coach. A mentor often turns into a great friend. If a leader isn't coaching, then he isn't doing his job.

Without friendship and mentorship in the workplace, there is no great leadership. Leadership is built upon and supported by the relationships established through workplace friendships and mentorships. Absent strong leadership, employees have 'jobs' rather than a passion and a commitment, and companies are left with revolving doors of talent. Revolving doors are expensive to maintain.

If you have ever seen an episode of the reality television show "Undercover Boss," then you know what I mean. The show starts with the CEO of a company who joins employees on the front lines, getting to know firsthand what they do daily to be successful and to make the company successful. Sometimes they learn that the people working the front lines know more about what it takes to make the company successful than the people sitting in the C-suite.

In its eighth season, the CEO of mega women's fashion retailer New York & Company, Greg Scott, went undercover. He started his first day in Bensalem, Pennsylvania, working as a sales associate during the closing shift.

Scott knew that sales associates make the difference between a good store and a great store. On that first shift working with Anthony, a sales associate, Greg learned how certain company policies made it difficult for the customer to understand prices, and a lack of training made it difficult for employees to effectuate a great customer experience. He also learned about the dress code differences for men and women that didn't seem logical, such as limiting the colors they're allowed to wear.

As soon as the shift ended and the store closed, Anthony and Greg were dressing mannequins. Greg said, "So tell me a little bit about yourself." Anthony then explained to Greg that his mother died when he was a kid, his father wasn't really in the picture, and his grandparents raised him. He shared his hopes and dreams for finishing college and working in fashion. Greg noted Anthony had an eye for it, and the company needed more associates like him.

The next day, Greg went to Wyomissing, Pennsylvania, to work with a fitting room stylist, Amber. Amber told him that she hears from many younger women who walk in but perceive the store to be for older women; they aren't interested. He asked her if she would ever be a manager. Amber explained she had a two-year-old child, and it wasn't easy. Her wedding was put on hold, because she and her fiancé didn't have enough money to pay for the wedding *and* take care of a child. She told Greg she had the drive to succeed but needs to be patient. Greg was so impressed by her maturity, demeanor, and drive. "She's the total package," he said, and she was only twenty-two years old.

On the third day, Greg went to Fayetteville, North Carolina, to work with a stock person. Organization and processing are critical for sales success. The stock room was in disarray when he arrived, and the sales floor had multiple empty shelves. Greg met Panya, who explained that each piece of clothing must be removed from the box, tagged with a security sensor and placed in the correct spot. Importantly, each box had a time indicator, telling the stock person exactly how long it should take her to completely empty the box and tag each item.

Panya explained that the store manager was out on maternity leave. The lightbulb went off in Greg's head. He knew immediately that the team at that store was lacking leadership. They were lacking the direction and guidance they needed to stay on track and make the store beautiful every day. In fact, Panya almost quit – twice – because the store was in such disarray.

"Why did you start doing this?" Greg asked. Panya explained she had been out of work for a while. Her daughter had leukemia, and she needed to care for her. Panya had a great work ethic and a desire to do her job well. Greg knew the company needed more Panyas.

The pivotal moment in the show came when Greg said, "Hearing about my employees' lives and their children and their parents made me think about how dedicated my dad was when my parents divorced. *There was such a connection there.*"

That's the power of workplace relationships. Greg learned *who* his employees were in addition to *what* they did to effectuate the company's strategy.

The epiphany didn't come to Greg after spending weeks and weeks on the front lines. He spent a few hours with each person, and built – in his own words – a connection. In building this connection with his employees, Greg learned key business needs, such as changes to the security tagging process, changes to dress codes, marketing to attract younger women, and more employee training and education.

Was the company doing well before "Undercover Boss"? Absolutely. Does the company have the potential to still do better? To *be* better? Yes.

With the former, leadership was standing alone; friendship and mentorship were not in the picture. With the latter, Greg put in motion the small steps it takes to build friendships. Greg put that in motion when he formed meaningful connections, connections that reminded him of his own family. He planted the seeds of mentorship by sharing the potential he saw in each of his employees and helping to set them on a path of personal and professional development.

For every great tale of frientorship, there is a cautionary tale of frientorship being misapplied. Take Anne, for example. Anne was a very busy senior executive reporting to the CEO of a multi-billion-dollar company. Her days were scheduled well in advance with back-to-back meetings. In fact, she had to ask her assistant to block time for her to use the restroom. This might sound familiar to you. If it does, pay close attention.

Regardless of her hectic schedule, Anne was committed to having an open door and being available to any member of her 1,000-person team. That meant Anne scheduled time to coach the employees working the manufacturing line, those packaging products, those responsible for sales and marketing, as well as her senior leadership team.

Relationships mattered to Anne. Knowing and understanding her people mattered to Anne. Mentoring mattered to Anne. All of this is great. But there was a problem.

Anne was spending so much time on the friendship and mentorship levels that she wasn't doing enough to fulfill her leadership responsibilities. She thought she was doing that by spending time investing in employees all across her organization, and her cause and determination were noble for sure. She was doing so, however, at the expense of the people in the company who needed her the most: her direct reports.

Anne's calendar was so full that when her direct reports needed her, they had to wait days or even up to two weeks to be able to connect. Plus, in spending a large amount of time coaching and developing entry- and mid-level employees, Anne was actually depriving mid- and senior-level leaders of the opportunity to further develop their leadership skills and coach their own team members.

Anne had the best intentions. As Greg demonstrated, it is critical for CEOs and executives to spend time talking to and learning about all employees. This time, however, must be purposeful in both quantity and scope. Saying yes to every request leads to inevitable outcomes: priorities get missed, key business strategies are not executed, and business goals are not achieved. Mid- and senior-level leaders become frustrated and distracted. Even leaders with high levels of self-awareness can be blinded from time to time by their desire to be *liked*.

The important thing is that when offered feedback, Anne decided to pivot rather than dig in her heels. Hearing that her team felt neglected, Anne took a different approach that allowed her to be there for her team and to stay connected to the front lines. Anne established a program called, "Breakfast with Anne." Every other month, Anne blocked off two hours to have breakfast with entry- and mid-level employees. Anne spent thirty minutes doing a short but purposeful training program. The remainder of time was used as an open forum to discuss concerns as well as share success stories.

"Breakfast with Anne" sessions gave employees a chance to build a posse and connect with co-workers with whom they might not otherwise connect. It also gave them a chance to get to know a senior executive. Anne was able to keep her finger on the pulse of her organization while also doing what she loved – coaching and training. The sessions brought friendship and mentorship to life in a purposeful way that respected Anne's time and reflected her commitment to a large organization.

Most importantly, Anne was able to free up almost twenty – *twenty* – hours each month that she previously spent in one-on-one meetings with employees who reported to other leaders. Her direct reports had access to Anne once again, and their team members once again sought them out for coaching and development.

One or two hours a day committed to one thing doesn't seem like much... until you stop doing that one thing. Anne shared learnings with her direct reports during their team meeting, which enabled them to follow up with the individuals who needed more development. Anne's leadership team fostered mentorships and developed friendship, thereby setting them up for a better chance of leadership success.

Greg and Anne exemplify for us that friendship – getting to know *who* your employees or co-workers are – brings humanity into the workplace. We remember that people have families and bills to pay, and that each of us is struggling or has struggled in some way or another.

Mentorship – giving someone the time and the tools to get better – helps ensure the success of not one but two people. It's never too late to build or rebuild the strong foundation. In doing so, leaders rise above, and they find themselves able to leave in place leaders who are ready to take the reins when the time is right. That should be the mission of every CEO around the world.

FRIENTORSHIP FACTS

♦ Know what a day-in-the-life of every employee in your organization looks like.

♦ Remember that your employees are human beings who have responsibilities, bills to pay and families who depend on them.

♦ Bring humanity back into the workplace by implementing the principles of frientorship.

CHAPTER 11

FRIENTORSHIP ON FIRE

Success isn't a result of spontaneous combustion. You must set yourself on fire.

~ Arnold Glasow

Frientorship is lighter fluid. Now that you know what it is and what it looks like in action, it's time to strike a match and set it on fire in your organization. Are you ready to accept the challenge?

Start building your leadership legacy, one relationship at a time, focused on the future and the engaged people you someday will leave behind. After all, isn't that what it's all about? Legacy?

The meaning of legacy struck me as I was staring at my father's obituary, reading it for probably the one-millionth time:

Having been born on August 25, 1935, I lived a personally fulfilling life until Saturday, July 23, 2016 . . . I was, however, reborn several times. 1st time – June 1963; second time – October 1965; 3rd time – May 1970; 4th time October 1974. I will always be with my four daughters, their three husbands, whom I considered my sons, and my five grandchildren . . . The legacy I leave to the living world is my four educated daughters. They are a credit to themselves, their families, their professions and to the communities where they reside and work. Peace and good health forever.

An obituary – the résumé of your life. Professional résumés help people get jobs, but obituaries (a.k.a. life résumés) – they tell our story after we're done living it.

Think about all the obituaries you have read. Have you ever come across an obituary written in first person and in present tense? In the days and hours leading to his death, the death he knew was coming but did not want, my father did just that.

He wrote his obituary in first person, focused on the future. He didn't write a single word about what he – Frank Moreno – had done. In fact, he wrote very little about the past, referring to the births of his four children as times of his own rebirth.

He was focused on his legacy. His children. His *team*. What made him great was not how he was the first in his family to go to college or how he owned his own business or the awards he won as a young man, or how much money he made, or anything else that he, personally, accomplished. What made him great was how he trained and nurtured and developed his *team* to be able to rise up and lead our family when he stopped being our leader.

My dad had a unique ability to be our friend when we needed a friend, our mentor when we needed to learn something, and the proverbial patriarch of an Italian-American family, a leader to all those on life's journey with him. He wasn't perfect, of course, but he did his best. Most importantly, he did everything he could to tee his daughters up for their own success and to carry on the family name and traditions. That is frientorship on fire.

Just as my dad imparted that wisdom unto me, so can a leader in an organization. Leaders who focus not just on their own success but rather on the success of their teams inevitably drive their own success and the success of the entire organization. It is through striving to make others successful that we make ourselves more successful.

If the principles of frientorship are leveraged in Corporate America, employees and businesses alike will thrive. Unlike the cost of other *things* companies are buying to coax employees to deliver results, building great workplace relationships through frientorship does not cost a lot of money. And while the things Corporate America is buying are often necessary and have great potential to drive engagement, they will not achieve success without the human connection they need to thrive.

Once your organization learns how to implement frientorship, the process will be self-sustaining, cascading down from leader to team and sideways from peer to peer and so on.

Best of all, the cascade won't cost a penny.

ACKNOWLEDGMENTS

I am so grateful to the people who have been there for me over the years, through career changes and life changes. Without them, this book never would have come to fruition.

First and foremost, thank you to my dad, Frank Moreno, in heaven. I wish I could still talk to him and that he could see the great things his grandchildren are doing. Without the lessons he taught me, the concept of frientorship would not have been realized. He will always be the ultimate leader in my life.

Thank you to my mom, Coral "Cookie" Moreno, also in heaven. I'm certain I will never be as good a cook as she, but I promise to do my best to pass her recipes on to my girls. I didn't appreciate it at the time, but I now understand how hard she worked to have amazing, home-cooked meals on the table every night so we could have a family dinner.

My sisters, Elisa Moreno, Suzanne Vercruysse, and Amy Moreno. The best friends I know I will ever have, even though we drive each other crazy. Whether it's up, down, or sideways, we always end up with family over everything. We can say whatever we want to each other, but we will defend each other to the death if others attack. #pistachio

Thanks to my Chocolate Posse: Lauren Lacey, Lois Duquette, and Jennifer Shugars. From lunchtime movie breaks to office tears to happy hours to constant text messages... my career and life wouldn't be the same without you.

John Dame, who coached me, believed in me, and kept pushing me. He brought me into the most amazing Vistage posse where I was able to build great relationships, develop my skills, and make great friends (Jeff, Joe, Kevin, Kellee, Julie, Tracey and so many more).

Jayne Huston, who started as my coach and became my friend. She traveled near and far to support me, and I am so grateful.

Kim Cole and Amanda Lavis – the greatest people and friends. Each of them has been there for me at different times in my life and career journey, and they stood by me through it all. They inspire me to be better. They bring the frientorship idea to life. Thank you.

Thank you to Henry DeVries for getting me started on this book journey.

Thank you to Demi Stevens for bringing the book journey home and for the great food prepared for me during the days we buckled down to get this done!

Thank you to everyone who made this book possible and who brings frientorship to life for me each day. Thank you to the clients who gave me a chance. Thank you to those who came before me and inspired me to pursue my passion and who reinforced that my line of thinking was not totally crazy (like Brené Brown, Angela Duckworth, Shawn Achor, and so many more). If your name isn't listed, it doesn't mean you haven't had an impact on my life. It means I'm an idiot for not listing you.

ABOUT THE AUTHOR

The youngest of four girls, Claudia's dad nicknamed her "Clyde" and taught her to fish and golf. After seemingly endless summers on the golf course with her dad, she went to Penn State and became a member of the Women's Varsity Golf Team. She began her career as an Assistant Golf Professional. Seeking more fulfillment, she decided to follow her other dream of becoming a lawyer. After law school, she landed a job with a top international law firm and later became an equity partner at a different firm. From private practice, she joined The Hershey Company as Associate General Counsel, Global HR & Litigation. (Yes, endless supplies of chocolate were a perk!)

She received the 2015 Pennsylvania Bar Association Special Achievement Award in recognition of her pro-bono commitment to veterans and first responders. She was named as one of the Central Penn Business Journal's 25 Women of Influence and was named as one of Philadelphia Magazine's Super Lawyers multiple times. Claudia was nominated for the Business Women's Forum Business Woman of the Year award in 2017.

In 2015, Claudia decided to take her lawyer hat off and start her own consulting business, The Human Zone. She now works with organizations of all sizes to transform leaders and build great places to work.

Claudia serves as a member of the Advisory Board for The Salvation Army Harrisburg Capital City Region, where she also co-chairs and helped found the Shoe Strut, an annual fundraiser for TSA. Because of the Shoe Strut, thousands of local children in need have received new shoes, and tens of thousands of dollars have been raised to support TSA programs and services.

She lives in Central Pennsylvania with her husband, Steve, and their two, spirited daughters, building family memories and legacies to last for lifetimes to come.

WORK WITH THE AUTHOR

KEYNOTE ADDRESS:

Frientorship can come to life and plant the seeds of inspiration in a powerful keynote address. Over the course of one hour, attendees leave feeling energized and inspired to think about work and life a little differently. They return to work and share the inspiration with those around them. It's a win-win for companies, associations and events looking for a fresh, energizing perspective to share.

HALF-DAY, FULL-DAY AND TWO-DAY WORKSHOPS:

All frientorship workshops have interactive components, getting the audience to think and engage in real time. You can't sit there on your electronic device and pretend to pay attention. You need to do some work. You need to be present. Teams need to do work together. Collectively, we learn. We share. We grow. We prosper.

ONE-ON-ONE VIP COACHING:

We use a variety of tools to help leaders cultivate relationships, increase self-awareness, reconnect with their teams and deliver business results. Coaching is targeted to meet the development needs of the individual. Using a combination of data and first-hand information, we prioritize pain points and formulate a plan to address each one. Is it easy? No. Behavior is one of the most difficult things to change. Is it worth it? Yes. Remember Anne? It saved her job, her career, and her team.

Contact the author to learn more about your frientorship options.

Share your stories of frientorship success!

[in] www.linkedin.com/in/claudiamwilliams

[f] ww.facebook.com/ClaudiaWilliamsFrientor

[t] www.twitter.com/HumanZoneBiz

THE 3 QUESTIONS YOU MUST ASK EVERY TIME YOU MEET WITH A MEMBER OF YOUR TEAM

These three questions guarantee that you will have your finger on the pulse of your team. If you know how the people on your team are feeling, then you know how they are performing. If you know how they are performing, you are able to coach them appropriately.

Visit www.frientorship.com/tools to start asking the most important questions *today*.

NOTES

NOTES

NOTES